CB128317

B1+
WORKBOOK

BEYOND

MACMILLAN

Andy Harvey
Louis Rogers

Macmillan Education
4 Crinan Street
London N1 9XW
A division of Macmillan Publishers Limited

Companies and representatives throughout the world

ISBN 978-0-230-46020-1

Written by Andy Harvey and Louis Rogers
The authors have asserted their rights to be identified as the authors of this work in accordance with the Copyright, Designs and Patents Act 1988.

First published 2015

Designed by emc design ltd
Illustrated by Stephen Dew pp 100, 122; Kev Hopgood pp 34, 39, 58, 80, 88; Bob Lea p 116 (3D printer).
Cover design by emc design ltd
Cover photographs by Alamy/Tim Gainey, Alamy/Frans Lemmens
Picture research by Lorraine Beck

The authors and publishers would like to thank the following for permission to reproduce their photographs:

Alamy/Alliance p56(3), Alamy/Simon Belcher p119, Alamy/Brendan Bell p26(3), Alamy/BSIP SA p7, Alamy/Caro pp64(8d), 66(c), Alamy/ClassicStock p86(t), Alamy/Cristina Fumi pp64(2d), 68(bcr), Alamy/Ray Grover p64(9a), Alamy/Jim Holden p89(r), Alamy/Ingram Publishing p64(3d), Alamy/Kuzma p95(l), Alamy/david pearson pp31, 40(10), 116(a), Alamy/Photofusion Picture Library pp64(7a), 66(f), Alamy/pixelbully p16(6) Google and the Google logo are registered trademarks of Google Inc., used with permission, Alamy/Radius Images pp64(6d), 68(tr); **Barcroft Media via Getty Images** p10; **Bloomberg via Getty Images** pp20(c), 64(5a), 66(e); **Corbis**/Fabrice Lerouge/Onoky p95(r), Corbis/Don Mason p40(5), Corbis/Ocean/Daniel Allan p21, Corbis/Trish Punch/Design Pics pp64(2a), 66(b), Corbis/Tomas Rodriguez p23, Corbis/Oliver Rossi p68(b), Corbis/Qilai Shen/epa p116(b), Corbis/viewpress Vp/Demotix p81, Corbis/Nick White/Image Source p56(1); **Fotolibra**/Derek Metson pp64(1d), 66(d); **Francisco de Pájaro** pp54, 56(4); **Getty Images**/Peter Beavis p44(4), Getty Images/Juliet Coombe p60, Getty Images/Brian Cooper p33(t), Getty Images/Sean Davey p26(7), Getty Images/Michael DeLeon p4(2), Getty Images/Dorling Kindersley p52(ml), Getty Images/Sam Edwards p40(9), Getty Images/franckreporter p46, Getty Images/Timothy Hiatt p66(b), Getty Images/Hill Street Studios p44(3), Getty Images/Steve Mason p20(e), Getty Images/OFurrer OFurrer p26(1), Getty Images/Photodisc p77, Getty Images/Picturenet p114, Getty Images/Frank Rothe p17, Getty Images/William Sallaz p4(8), Getty Images/Chris Schmidt p91, Getty Images/Thomas_EyeDesign p26 (9), Getty Images/Ethan Welty p52(mr), Getty Images/Westend61 pp40(7), 71, Getty Images/Simon Winnall p107(b);

Macmillan Publishers Ltd pp76, 83(letter), Macmillan Publishers Ltd/Bananastock p107(e), Macmillan Publishers Ltd/Brand X pp28(10), 30, 40(1), 59(b), 65(l), 96, 115, Macmillan Publishers Ltd/Corbis pp4(7), 5(4), 59(a), 65(r), Macmillan Publishers Ltd/Creatas p40(8), Macmillan Publishers Ltd/DigitalStock/Corbis p53, Macmillan Publishers Ltd/Digital Vision p29, Macmillan Publishers Ltd/Getty Images pp4(1, 4), 26(8, 12), 28(8), 33(b), 35(tl), 84(t), 102, 113(tr), Macmillan Publishers Ltd/image100 pp35(cm), 47(3), Macmillan Publishers Ltd/ImageSource pp11, 22, 26(2), 40(11), 43, 47(1), 49, 92, 101, 103, 110(t), 120, Macmillan Publishers Ltd/ImageState p26(5), Macmillan Publishers Ltd/Macmillan Australia pp26(10), 28(12), 35(cl), 40(4), 108, Macmillan Publishers Ltd/Macmillan Education/Stuart Cox p16(5), Macmillan Publishers Ltd/Macmillan New Zealand p35(tr), Macmillan Publishers Ltd/PhotoAlto p117, Macmillan Publishers Ltd/Photodisc pp5(b), 35(cr), 94, 118(b), 122, Macmillan Publishers Ltd/Photodisc/Getty Images pp28(2, 7, 11), 40(2), 56(2), p83(banknotes), p84(b), 105, p112(t, b), Macmillan Publishers Ltd/Photodisc/Getty Images/Linda Bronson p55, Macmillan Publishers Ltd/Pixtal p65(m), Macmillan Publishers Ltd/Purestock/Punchstock/Getty Images p26(4), Macmillan Publishers Ltd/Rubber Ball p40(6), Macmillan Publishers Ltd/Stockbyte p83(parcel), Macmillan Publishers Ltd/Thinkstock pp16(2, 3), 28(5, 9), 38, 41, 47(2), p59(c, d), p89(l), 104, 110(b), 111; **plainpicture**/applypictures p69, plainpicture/TatjaB. pp64(4d), 66(a), 68(tcr); **REX**/Steve Black p79; **Science Photo Library**/US Geological Survey p113(bl); **Superstock**/View Pictures Ltd p118(t); **Thinkstock**/Fabio Alcini p14(1), Thinkstock/Helder Almeida p12, Thinkstock/Artranq p86(b), Thinkstock/ASIFE p19 , Thinkstock/Brand X Pictures p32, Thinkstock/Hanquan Chen p16(4), Thinkstock/Comstock Images pp8(4), 57(r), Thinkstock/Creatas p15, Thinkstock/crisod p26(11), Thinkstock/decisiveimages p67, Thinkstock/Michel de Nijs p4(6), Thinkstock/EduardHarkonen p14(4), Thinkstock/Greg Epperson p8(1), Thinkstock/ep stock p20(b), Thinkstock/evgenyatamanenko p16(1), Thinkstock/Fuse p20(d), Thinkstock/Nikhil Gangavane p14(6),Thinkstock/Sean Gladwell p14(3), Thinkstock/grapix p5(1), Thinkstock/Svetlana Gryankina p14(7), Thinkstock/Hemera Technologies p57(l), Thinkstock/Jonathan Hill p4(5), Thinkstock/Hill Street Studios p5(2), Thinkstock/Jack Hollingsworth p107(c), Thinkstock/jsolem p52(l), Thinkstock/Jupiterimages p20(f), Thinkstock/kanyakits p44(2), Thinkstock/Lonely__ p44(1), Thinkstock/Mallivan p107(g), Thinkstock/Maridav p72, Thinkstock/Tony Marven p107(a), Thinkstock/Adrian Matthiassen p8(3), Thinkstock/Davis McCardle p28(3), Thinkstock/Ryan McVay p74, Thinkstock/mettus p107(d), Thinkstock/miflippo p14(5), Thinkstock/monkeybusinessimages p40(12), Thinkstock/Domenico Pellegriti p28(4), Thinkstock/Pinosub p4(3), Thinkstock/Purestock p9, Thinkstock/RickBL p5(3), Thinkstock/Giovanni Rinaldi p14(8), Thinkstock/Joseph Ruscigno p42, Thinkstock/satori13 p28(6), Thinkstock/sedmak p52(r), Thinkstock/Stockbyte p14(2), Thinkstock/TPopova p13, Thinkstock/underworld111 p35(br), Thinkstock/Wavebreakmedia Ltd pp40(3), 107(f), Thinkstock/weareadventurers p20(a), Thinkstock/Karl Weatherly pp8(2), 26(6), Thinkstock/Roland Zihlmann p28(1)

Printed and bound in Thailand

2019 2018 2017 2016 2015
11 10 9 8 7 6 5 4 3

CONTENTS

1 BE EXTREME!

UNIT

VOCABULARY 1 >>> Talk about different adventure sports

1 a Label the photos of sports and activities.

1 t _ _ _ _ s

2 h _ _ _ _ y

3 w _ _ _ r p _ _ o

4 s _ _ _ _ g

5 b _ _ _ _ _ _ _ _ l

6 s _ _ _ _ _ _ g

7 b _ _ _ _ g

8 w _ _ _ _ _ _ g

b How many of the sports in Exercise 1a can you do alone? ________

2 Match the words to make the names of the adventure sports.

1	sky	a	boarding	*snowboarding*
2	free	b	surfing	________
3	ice	c	gliding	________
4	snow	d	climbing	________
5	skate	e	diving	________
6	body	f	surfing	________
7	hang	g	boarding	________
8	wind	h	running	________

3 Choose the correct option to complete the sentences.

1 I go rock ***jumping*** / ***climbing*** every Saturday in winter.
2 Do you want to come base ***jumping*** / ***boarding*** tonight?
3 Jan's entered a free ***diving*** / ***surfing*** competition.
4 I love bungee ***diving*** / ***jumping*** , don't you?
5 Tower ***jumping*** / ***running*** sounds very tiring to me.
6 Mountain ***riding*** / ***biking*** isn't much fun in the rain.

4 a Look at the key below and draw the correct arrow(s) next to each sport.

Sports that involve going up ︿
Sports that involve going down ﹀
Sports that involve going along 〉
Sports that involve going up, down and along ︿ ﹀ 〉

1 skydiving ﹀
2 skiing ________
3 bungee jumping ________
4 tower running ________
5 skateboarding ________
6 snowboarding ________
7 mountain biking ________

b Write the names of two adventure sports that you would like to try.

________ ________

5 Find and write the words in the word search.

1 two words for frozen water: i *c* e, s _ _ w
2 four words for moving down: s _ _ _ e, d _ _ e
j _ _ p, f _ _ l
3 two words for high places: c _ _ _ f, h _ _ l

E	P	B	F	F	A	F	E	G	Y
H	C	Z	J	F	O	U	D	A	V
M	F	I	H	I	U	Y	I	L	E
P	C	D	U	L	X	Z	L	P	G
L	L	A	F	C	F	H	S	P	A
C	O	S	S	H	K	T	G	M	Y
S	N	O	W	E	I	N	H	U	B
P	T	H	G	N	V	L	Q	J	W
G	V	Z	K	E	M	I	L	U	R
N	J	S	N	D	D	P	D	J	L

6 Complete the email with the words in the box.

climb equipment extreme
protective speeds surfing

Hi Jamal,

I'm sending you a link to an amazing video of this (1) ________ sport called volcano (2) ________ . I suppose it's like snowboarding – the only (3) ________ you need is a board and some (4) ________ clothing because you can really reach some very high (5) ________ . The problem is that it can be a long (6) ________ up to the top. Check it out!

See you,

Al

READING

Recognise and understand idioms

1 Complete the tips with the words in the box.

REMEMBER HOW TO …

recognise and understand idioms

clues image meaning obvious text understand

- Look for expressions where the (1) ………… isn't (2) ………… .
- Look for (3) ………… before or after the idiom to help you (4) ………… .
- Think about how the (5) ………… in the idiom relates to the (6) ………… .

2 Look at the photos. Rearrange the words in bold to make an idiom for each situation.

1 

2 

3 

4 

1 I think you should start with something easier. **off / more / chew / than / bite / can / you / Don't / .**
Don't bite off more than you can chew.

2 I don't like classical music. **my / tea / cup / not / of / It's / .**
…………

3 I'm sure I can do this easily. **up / right / street / It's / my / .**
…………

4 We'll never win this match. **cause / It's / lost / a / .**
…………

3 Choose the correct options to complete the conversation.

Alex: Do you know what?
George: What?
Alex: You can be a real pain in the (1) ***head*** / ***neck*** sometimes.
George: Why?
Alex: We have the chance to go bungee jumping and you don't want to (2) ***have*** / ***do*** a go.
George: Well, jumping off bridges or towers with an elastic cord tied around my feet just isn't my cup of (3) ***coffee*** / ***tea*** , I'm afraid. I don't have a head for heights.
Alex: It's not just that. You run a (4) ***metre*** / ***mile*** from anything that involves adventure or taking a risk, don't you?
George: Alex, look, doing dangerous things is something right up your (5) ***street*** / ***road*** , but it's really not for me. Go ahead and do stuff by yourself if you want.
Alex: George, you're a lost (6) ***cause*** / ***reason*** . I'm not going on holiday with you again.

4 a Read the conversation in Exercise 3 again and decide if the statements are True (*T*), False (*F*) or Not stated (*NS*).

1 Alex is annoyed with George. T/F/NS
2 George likes danger. T/F/NS
3 George prefers coffee to tea. T/F/NS
4 George runs long distances. T/F/NS
5 Alex is told that he can do things alone. T/F/NS
6 Alex wants to go on holiday with George again. T/F/NS

b Which activity is right up your street?

…………

5 a Read the email. Which sport do you think Katrin will choose?

…………

19:30

Hi Avril,
I want to do something physical and need your advice. What I want is a sport that doesn't *cost an arm and a leg* and something that I can *get the hang of* quite quickly. That means skydiving is *out of the question!* Anyway, I don't have *a head for heights*. I'm *in two minds* between skateboarding and mountain biking. My dad says I've *got my head in the clouds* if I think he'll buy me the expensive bike that *caught my eye*, so perhaps the best choice is to get a skateboard. What do you think?
Katrin

b Match the idioms in *italics* in the text to the meanings (1–7). Write the idiom on the answer line.

1 definitely not a possibility …………
2 have difficulty making a decision …………
3 not like being high up …………
4 be expensive …………
5 be noticed …………
6 learn to do something (well) …………
7 not think in a realistic way …………

GO BEYOND

Use the internet to find an article in English about *extreme ironing*. Use the tips in Exercise 1 to help you understand it.

GRAMMAR 1 Present tenses review

>>> Talk about things happening now and things that are generally true

1 Complete the grammar tables with the correct forms.

A Present simple – positive				
I/You/We/ (1)		usually train		at the gym twice a day.
He/ (2)		often (3)		at the gym.
Present simple – negative				
I/You/We/They		(4) ...... train		at a gym.
He/ (5)		(6)		
Present simple – questions				**Answers**
When	(7)	I/you/we/they	(8) ...... ?	Twice a week.
	(9)	she/he	train?	Every day.
Present simple – *yes/no* questions				**Answers**
Do	I/you/we/they	(10)	at a gym?	Yes, I do. No, they (11) ....
(12)	she/he			Yes, she does. No, he (13) ....

B Present continuous – positive (negative)			
I	(1) ...... (not)	playing basketball	at the moment.
He/She	(2) ...... (not)		right now.
You/We/They	(3) ...... (not)		now.
Present continuous – *yes/no* questions			**Answers**
(4)	I	learning anything here?	Yes, I am.
(5)	he/she		No, he/she isn't.
(6)	you/we/they		No, we/you/they aren't.

C Present simple passive – positive (negative)		
I	(1) ...... (not)	invited to the big party.
He/She	(2) ...... (not)	
You/We/They	(3) ...... (not)	
Present simple passive – questions		**Answers**
Am I	invited to the big party?	No, I (4) ....
Is he/she		Yes, he/she (5) ....
Are you/we/they		No, you/we/they (6) ....

2 Choose the correct option to complete the rules. Use the tables in Exercise 1 to help you.

1. Use the present ***simple* / *continuous*** to talk about habits, routines or things that are generally true.
2. Use the present ***simple* / *continuous*** to talk about things happening now or around now.
3. We often use adverbs and expressions of frequency (eg *sometimes, rarely, every day*) with the present ***simple* / *continuous***.
4. State verbs (eg *believe, understand, like*) are rarely used with the present ***simple* / *continuous***.
5. Use the present simple passive when the person or thing that does the action is unknown, or when the action is ***less* / *more*** important than the person or thing that does the action.

3 Write the third person singular of the verbs in the box in the correct column (-s, -es or -*ies*).

do ~~feel~~ go play
study train try work

-s	-es	-ies
feels		

4 › **Complete the sentences with the verbs in Exercise 3. Use each verb once only.**

Sue (1) ________ wheelchair tennis on Sunday mornings with Jo. Their coach (2) ________ them for an hour and then they have a game. Sue is 18 and (3) ________ maths at college, and Jo is 19 and (4) ________ in a call centre. Jo regularly (5) ________ skydiving and never (6) ________ better than when she's up in the clear blue sky. She (7) ________ hard at everything she (8) ________ . That's true for Sue too.

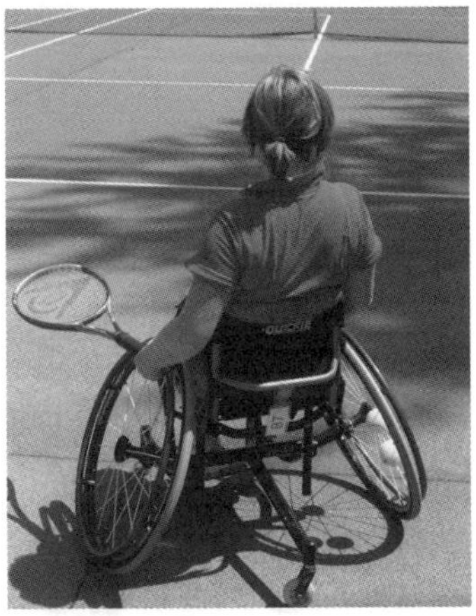

5 › **Write one more verb next to each category of state verbs. Use the words in the box.**

hate hear look own understand

1 mental states and opinions, eg *know, believe,* ________
2 preferences, eg *like, need,* ________
3 appearance, eg *seem, appear,* ________
4 possession, eg *belong, include,* ________
5 senses, eg *taste, smell,* ________

6 › **Choose the correct options to complete the text.**

I (1) ___ if (2) ___ to start the game. I usually (3) ___ on as a sub in the second half and I often (4) ___ a goal in the final minutes. I (5) ___ that I can add that something extra and when we (6) ___ and there's ten minutes to the final whistle, I (7) ___ to get that adrenaline rush and just (8) ___ the ball to show what I can do.

	a	b	c
1	a don't care	b 'm not caring	c 'm not cared
2	a I'm not picking	b I don't pick	c I'm not picked
3	a come	b 'm come	c 'm coming
4	a 'm scoring	b 'm scored	c score
5	a know	b 'm known	c 'm knowing
6	a lose	b 're losing	c 're lost
7	a 'm seemed	b seem	c 'm seeming
8	a 'm wanting	b 'm wanted	c want

7 »› **Rearrange the words to make questions.**

1 go / often / snowboarding / you / do / ?
Do you often go snowboarding?
2 team / these days / is / doing well / your / ?
____
3 the players / who's / are / told / in the team / when / ?
____
4 sports wheelchair / does / every / the same / look / ?
____
5 currently / you / are / for any / training / particular competition / ?
____
6 the racket / by Andy Murray / used / is / that / ?
____

8 »› **Correct the mistakes in bold.**

Igor: (1) **Does** young people always **be wanting to pushed** the limits?
Do young people always want to push the limits?

Ivana: (2) I'm not sure what **are you meaning**.
____

Igor: (3) They **is needing** to **be known** the rules, but enjoy the freedom to take risks.
____

Ivana: (4) So **are you thinking** that life **is being** a bit like playing sport then?
____

Igor: (5) It **is seeming** to me that in both you **are required** the confidence to have a go.
____

Ivana: (6) You **aren't** succeed all the time, but you **prepared** for the next challenge.
____

9 a »»› **Use the prompts to write questions. Use the present simple, present continuous or present simple passive.**

1 anyone / know / rules of cricket?
Does anyone know the rules of cricket?
2 you / remember / your first win?
____
3 Dennis / swim / at the moment?
____
4 what / be / the most extreme sport?
____
5 how often / you crash / your bike?
____
6 the players / tell / by the coach / train every day?
____

b Match the questions in Exercise 9a to the answers below.

___ a No. They have a day off on Sundays.
___ b No. They're too confusing.
___ c In my view, base jumping.
___ d Yes. I can see him in the pool.
___ e Of course I do. It was at the European windsurfing finals.
___ f Every time I go out on it, unfortunately.

LISTENING

>>> Take notes

1 Match the sentence halves to complete the tips.

REMEMBER HOW TO ...

take notes

- (1) Focus on ____ a the most important or interesting points.
- (2) Write down ____ b space between lines to add more detail later.
- (3) Use ____ c bullet points, abbreviations and symbols (*ie* = *in other words*, → = *leads to*).
- (4) Leave ____ d key words or very short sentences.

2 Label the photos of the extreme sports.

1 
2 
3 
4 

1 a________ 2 m________ b________ 3 h________-________ 4 k________

3 Which words in the box do you associate with each sport in Exercise 2? Write them in the correct column below. You can use the words more than once. Use your dictionary to check your answers.

cliff ☐	climb ☐	cross ☐	descend ☐	fall ☐
fly ☐	hillside ☐	land ☐	race ☐	river ☐
ropes ☐	summit ☐	tracks ☐	water ☐	wind ☐

Photo 1	Photo 2	Photo 3	Photo 4

4 ▶01 Listen to three short conversations and take note of the important information. Which of the sports from Exercise 2 were they doing?

CONVERSATION 1:
Notes: ________
Sport: ________

CONVERSATION 2:
Notes: ________
Sport: ________

CONVERSATION 3:
Notes: ________
Sport: ________

5 a ▶01 Listen again and tick (✓) any of the words from Exercise 3 that you hear.

b Rewrite the words in the correct conversation. Listen again if you need to.

Conversation 1: ________

Conversation 2: ________

Conversation 3: ________

6 a Complete the phrases from the conversations.

Conversation 1
1 as free as a ________
2 adrenaline ________
3 I felt like a ________
4 check all my ________

Conversation 2
5 How does it ________?
6 out of this ________

Conversation 3
7 to be ________
8 really rough ________

b ▶02 Now listen and check your answers.

VOCABULARY 2

Achievements and challenges

1 Choose the correct option (a, b or c) to complete the sentences.

1 You can't get to the top if you don't take ____ .
a attempts
b risks
c tasks

2 Nothing beats achieving your ____ .
a fears
b obstacles
c dreams

3 We have to ____ our problems and not run away from them.
a face
b achieve
c reach

4 I don't think I ____ my potential as a free diver.
a encountered
b fulfilled
c overcame

5 Why didn't you ____ the offer of a free skydiving course?
a risk
b reach
c take up

6 Just imagine a teenager ____ to circumnavigate the world alone!
a attempting
b taking
c reaching

7 Of course you'll ____ difficulties on this trip.
a achieve
b encounter
c fulfil

8 Jordan was on top of the world when he ____ the summit.
a overcame
b took up
c reached

2 Match the sentence halves.

1 Always check your equipment
2 This is all about
3 He did exceptionally well even though he failed this time, so
4 I took a chance
5 She faced her fear of heights and went
6 Do you think I'm going to
7 If you don't attempt difficult tasks,
8 What obstacles

a and it worked out well.
b overcoming difficulties.
c risk my life by jumping off a cliff?
d rock climbing.
e so you won't encounter problems with your ropes on the way down.
f did you have to overcome?
g I'm sure he will achieve his goals in the end.
h you can't get to the top.

WORDS & BEYOND

3 a Complete the phrases with the words in the box.

bench	fight	globe	kayaking	routine	shoulder	skyscraper	wave

1 ride a ____
2 put up a ____
3 circumnavigate the ____
4 tap someone on the ____
5 rehearse a new dance ____
6 sit on a ____
7 abseil down a ____
8 love going ____

b Name two adventure sports you need a parachute for.

____
____

GRAMMAR 2 Past tenses review

Talk about past achievements

1 Match the tenses (1–4) to their uses (a–d).

1 Past perfect simple (*had* + past participle) ____
2 Past simple (verb + *-ed*) ____
3 Past simple passive (*was/were* + past participle) ____
4 Past continuous (*was/were* + verb + *-ing*) ____

a For actions in progress in the past.
b For completed actions in the past.
c When the action is more important than the person/thing that did the action.
d To show that an action happened before another action or time in the past.

2 › Write the past simple and past participle forms of these irregular verbs.

	Past simple	Past participle
1 beat	beat	beat/beaten
2 become		
3 begin		
4 blow		
5 break		
6 buy		
7 cost		
8 cut		
9 fall		
10 feel		
11 find		
12 fly		

3 ›› Choose the correct options to complete the text.

In September 2013, Jonathan Trappe (1) ***attempted* / *was attempted*** to fly across the Atlantic solo, sitting in a small lifeboat hanging under 370 balloons. He (2) ***was* / *had*** already crossed the English Channel from England to France a few years earlier, in 2010, and he had previously (3) ***broken* / *broke*** the world record for the longest helium-filled balloon flight. The trip from America to Europe didn't (4) ***begin* / *begun*** well, and after only 12 hours he (5) ***was forced* / *forced*** to end the trip because of technical problems. The winds (6) ***were* / *had*** blowing him up and down, and he couldn't achieve the steady height of around 25,000 feet he (7) ***needed* / *was needing***. Eventually he (8) ***had landed* / *landed*** safely in the sea only 350 miles from where he (9) ***was taking* / *had taken*** off. Europe (10) ***was* / *was being*** still over two thousand miles away.

4 a ››› Complete the questions with the correct past form of the verbs in the box.

be (x2)	cross	do (x2)	fly (x2)	have	give	make	start	tell

1 D*id* you ever feel afraid when you were f*lying* over the sea?
2 When you first f______ with helium balloons, w______ you the first person to do that?
3 While you were c______ the Channel, what w______ you thinking?
4 Were you t______ by experts about the risks before you s______?
5 How far h______ you got before you g______ up?
6 What m______ you want to d______ it?

b Match the questions in Exercise 4a to the answers.

____ a I just remember saying to myself: 'It's so silent up here, and yet so beautiful.'
____ b Not really because I had a support and rescue team.
____ c I knew that it was dangerous, yes.
____ d I hadn't got anywhere near where I wanted to be.
____ e Well, nobody had ever done it before.
____ f I was told that I was, yes.

Start and change topics in a conversation

1 **03 Listen to the conversation. What event(s) are both girls going to at the weekend?**

....

....

2 **03 Listen again and read. Look at the underlined phrases (1–6). Decide whether each phrase is used to *start a new topic* (*A*), *change topic* (*B*) or *end the conversation* (*C*).**

Lou: Hi Kiki. (1) Did you know *A* that there's a skateboarding competition next weekend?

Kiki: Oh, really? Where?

Lou: At the shopping centre. Well, the park just outside, actually. Are you interested in taking part?

Kiki: Cool. When is it exactly? I can't do Saturday – homework and a party. (2) By the way, ... would you like to come?

Lou: To help you with the homework?

Kiki: Don't be silly! I mean to the party. A girl in my class, Laura, is 16. It's her birthday party.

Lou: Not Laura Moss?! I'm already invited. (3) Oh, that reminds me, ... I have to buy her a present. Do you have any ideas what to get?

Kiki: I don't know – something funny maybe. (4) Anyway, I've got to go. ...... (5) Oh, what about ...... the skateboarding competition?

Lou: Fortunately, that's on Sunday afternoon. Starts at four.

Kiki: Great. So, see you there.

Lou: And at Laura's. Looks like we're going to be seeing a lot of each other this weekend! (6) Bye for now. ......

3 **Complete the sentences with words in the box. There are three words you do not need to use. Don't worry about the numbers in brackets for now.**

go in know later look of remembers reminds talking to watch way

		(stressed syllables)
1	Oh, ... ! That's my bus.	(3)
2	I'm sorry, but I have to .... now.	(2)
3	Nice .... to you.	(2)
4	See you .... at the club.	(2)
5	That .... me, I need to go to the bank.	(4)
6	Talking .... extreme sports, would you like to try abseiling?	(4)
7	Did you .... that mountain biking is an Olympic sport?	(3)
8	By the .... , do the shops close early today?	(4)
9	Are you interested .... kayaking?	(2)

4 **a** **Practise saying the sentences in Exercise 3 out loud. Guess and underline the main stressed syllables (the number of stressed syllables is given in brackets). Here is an example:**

That reminds me. I need to go to the bank.
(4 stressed syllables)

b **04 Listen and check your answers. Then repeat.**

5 **a** **Write a short conversation using suitable phrases to start, change and end a conversation. You meet a friend and want to invite him/her to an event. He/She also wants to tell you some interesting news.**

A: ....
B: ....
A: ....
B: ....
A: ....
B: ....
A: ....
B: ....

b **Practise your conversation. Record it if you can.**

WRITING

Edit and proofread a text

1 Rewrite the sentences below to correct the spelling, punctuation, vocabulary and grammar mistakes in *italics*.

REMEMBER HOW TO …

edit and proofread a text

- Check the *long* and structure of *you're* work. Cut *every thing* that *is'nt* necessary.
- Check your *speling*, *punctuashion* and *using* of grammar especially.
- Then *carefuly* read your work a *finally* time to *checking* that it *make* sense. Or ask someone *other* to *reading* it.

Point 1: ....

....

Point 2: ....

....

Point 3: ....

....

2 Read the text. Do you think Max's ambition was to be famous, to be a writer or to be popular at school?

Max.a.million

Nobody believed it was me. To others I'd always been the quiet one, 'Sad Max'; the one who made excuses to avoid going to parties; the one who never joined in sports or took risks. In school I was the unpopular kid who sat at the back of the class trying not to be noticed – not easy due to my size. I'd never accomplished much either in my school studies or in anything else, but I did have one ambition I wanted to achieve, and secretly I was working at it. I'd signed up for a free course on the internet without even telling my parents and through that I learnt how to put words together to better express thoughts and feelings. I entered a poem in a junior national performance poetry competition on the theme of chance, and, well, I wanted to take my chance … I sent it in and read the poem at the final, which was filmed and now has thousands of views on YouTube. That's me! Really me! Max.a.million!

3 Is all the information necessary? Choose two sentences of at least 20 words and cross them out.

4 Read the entries written on Max.a.million's social network wall. Find and correct the mistakes.

1 Wow! That were an brilliant show.
That was a brilliant show.

2 You tells it like it is, brother!
....

3 That's the more amazing thing I've ever seen!
....

4 Do you having any more like this?
....

5 I has been told about this – now, after seeing it, I believe it … !
....

6 You is sounding so good.
....

WRITING PLAN

5 **You're going to write about an experience you had (or an imagined one) where you felt that you took a risk and it worked. Remember to use different tenses. Use the *Writing plan* to help you prepare.**

WRITING PLAN

Make notes for your story.

Describe ...

1 where and when the story happened. ☐

....

2 who was involved. ☐

....

....

3 why it was a risk. ☐

....

....

4 how you felt about it. ☐

....

....

5 what happened in the end. ☐

....

....

WRITE AND CHECK

6 a **Write about your experience and give your story a title. Then tick (✓) the stages in the *Writing plan*.**

b **Now reduce the length of your text by at least 20 words and check your spelling, punctuation, grammar and vocabulary.**

Consider the positive and negative aspects of taking risks

KNOW YOURSELF

1 **Complete the questionnaire for YOU. Put a tick (✓) in one column (*always*, *sometimes* or *never*).**

	ALWAYS	SOMETIMES	NEVER
1 I'm happy to eat something I've never eaten before.			
2 I've got my expensive mobile with me.			
3 I walk home alone at night.			
4 I accept invitations to parties.			
5 I do an extreme sport.			

2 **In your opinion, which three of the statements (1–5) in Exercise 1 involve the most risk? Why?**

1 Number ...... because ....

....

....

2 Number ...... because ....

....

....

3 Number ...... because ....

....

....

3 **Read the text and follow the instructions. Do you think this is a good way to decide things?**

Once, a man who found it difficult to make decisions decided that, for every decision, he'd write out six possible things he could do. Then, he would number them and throw a dice to let it tell him which choice to make. If the dice landed on six, he'd choose option six, and so on.

In your notebook, write a decision you have to make and a list of six choices for what you could do. Would you be brave (or stupid) enough to follow what the dice said?

1 Label the sports equipment.

1 r ....
2 s ....
3 b ....
4 s ....

5 s ....
6 p ....
7 r ....
8 s ....

2 Read the clues and complete the crossword with verbs of movement.

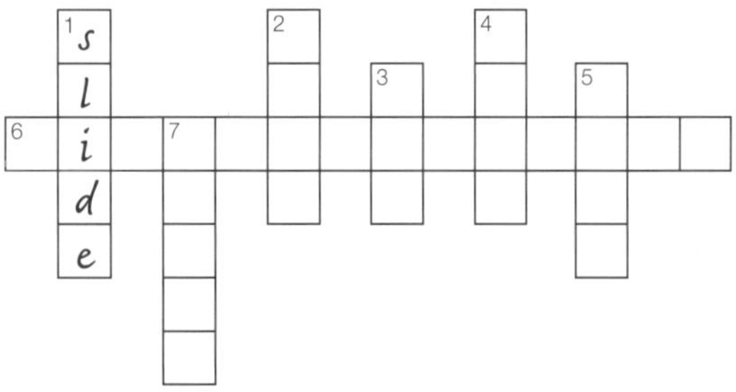

Down:

1 Snowboarders *slide* down the mountain.
2 Skydivers .... out of a plane to start a dive.
3 If you touch something lightly, you .... it.
4 To turn around and around in a circle is to ....
5 Everyone who does a base jump wants to .... safely!
7 Before you can abseil down, you have to .... up a rock or cliff.

Across:

6 To go all the way around the world is to .... the globe.

3 Match the sentence halves to make idioms.

1 Don't bite off
2 You can be a real pain
3 Doing dangerous sports isn't
4 I'd run
5 I tried to help him with his homework but then decided he was

a my cup of tea.
b a mile from anything that risks injury.
c a lost cause.
d more than you can chew.
e in the neck sometimes.

ALL ABOUT ME

1 What's your greatest achievement in life so far?

....

2 When have you been lucky in doing something?

....

3 Who has helped you most to achieve something? How did they help?

....

1 Choose the best options to complete the text.

Extreme experiments

A mad scientist (1) ____ the behaviour of the robot frogs he'd invented. He (2) ____ a frog on a flat surface and (3) ____ 'Jump' – and the frog (4) ____ . The scientist (5) ____ for his notebook and wrote, 'Frogs can jump'. Then, after he (6) ____ one of the frog's legs, he (7) ____ it to jump again. He wrote, 'Robot frogs can jump with one leg'. Then he (8) ____ the last leg and the frog (9) ____ to jump again. The scientist wrote, 'When robot frogs (10) ____ legs, they can't hear'.

	a	b	c
1	a was studied	b studying	c was studying
2	a put	b was put	c hadn't put
3	a was shouted	b had shouted	c shouted
4	a had	b did	c was
5	a reached	b was reaching	c didn't reach
6	a was removing	b was removed	c had removed
7	a had ordered	b ordered	c was ordering
8	a cut off	b cutting off	c had cut off
9	a told	b telling	c was told
10	a aren't having	b haven't got	c hadn't got

2 Complete the second sentence so that it has a similar meaning to the first. Use the word given. You should write between two and five words.

1 You have no idea of the beauty of being above the clouds.
understand
You *can't understand* the beauty that you feel when skydiving.

2 I fell from a cliff, but they found me.
rescued
I ____________ after falling from a cliff.

3 You can read the story online.
possible
It ____________ an online version of the story.

4 Was a European the first person to get to the North Pole?
been
Had ____________ reached by anyone before a European went there?

5 Does anybody know the true story?
real
Is ____________ by anybody?

6 Did anyone tell you about the risks?
informed
Were ____________ about the risks by anyone?

7 I don't enjoy any extreme sports.
tea
Extreme sports are ____________ .

3 Choose the correct options to complete the conversation.

Sam: Why (1) ***you didn't / didn't you*** answer me?
Paul: Because I (2) ***didn't hear / wasn't hearing*** my phone.
Sam: So, (3) ***don't you remember / aren't you remembering*** I told you about the game before?
Paul: Of course. (4) ***Are you thinking / Do you think*** I'm that forgetful?
Sam: Well, sometimes you can (5) ***be / do*** .
Paul: I haven't got time for this. (6) ***Are / Don't*** we going or not?
Sam: I (7) ***'ve / 'm having*** the tickets. Meet you outside gate number three at eight o'clock.

UNIT 2 DIGITAL FOOTPRINTS!

VOCABULARY 1 >>> Talk about using digital devices

1 Write the words to complete the sentences.

1 You u .... your photos to your website. [verb]
2 You c .... to the internet. [verb]
3 You sometimes s .... your credit card in the machine. [verb]
4 You s .... the internet to find something. [verb]
5 Your i .... is who you are. [noun]
6 You b .... the internet for fun. [verb]
7 You t .... an order to see when it will arrive. [verb]

2 Label the photos with the words in the box.

app camera map mobile
touch screen web browser

1 ....

2 ....

3 ....

4 ....

5 ....

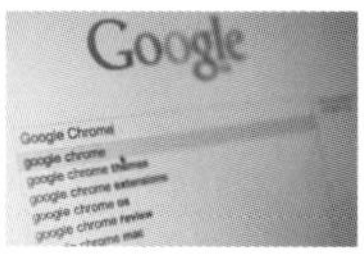

6 ....

3 What do these verbs relate to? Write them in the correct column. You can use the words more than once.

back up click download enter log on
log out scan set up turn down turn off
turn on turn up update upload

Machines	Computer Programs	Documents/ Files
turn off		

4 Complete the sentences with the words in the box.

back up download log out
swipe turn off turn up

1 Can you .... the volume, please? I can't hear it.
2 You have to remember to .... of your computer when you leave the office. Otherwise, people can access your emails and other personal information.
3 You should .... the computer when you're not using it to save energy.
4 I .... all my photos at least once a week as I don't want to lose them.
5 This music is taking forever to .... I need a faster internet connection.
6 Just .... your card there to pay.

5 Match the situations to the words in the box. Write them next to each speech bubble.

didn't click didn't enter didn't scan
didn't set up didn't update

This software is out of date. It isn't supported anymore. 1 ....

I forgot to type in my password, so I got an error message. 2 ....

My mouse wasn't working, so I couldn't select the option I wanted. 3 ....

I didn't create an account, so I can't use the service yet. 4 ....

The 3-in-1 printer in the office wasn't working, so I had to post the document. 5 ....

6 Complete the conversation with the words/ phrases in the box.

app camera download phone
scan set up track upload

Mo: Have you seen my new (1) .... ? It's got a 12 megapixel (2) ....
Ria: That's going to be so good when you want to (3) .... photos to the web.
Mo: It took me so long to (4) .... It was two hours before I could use it! Look at this.
Ria: What's that for?
Mo: I can use it to pay for things. You just (5) .... the code and then pay at the counter.
Ria: What if you lose it? Someone could go shopping with it or (6) .... your photos.
Mo: It's OK. This (7) .... lets me (8) .... my phone wherever it is. They might buy a few things but they'll soon get caught!

READING

Recognise main ideas and supporting points

1 Complete the sentences with the words in the box.

REMEMBER HOW TO …

recognise main ideas and supporting points

introduction   main idea   supporting points

- Identify the writer's opinion. Look in the (1) ________ or next paragraph.
- Look for one (2) ________ in each paragraph. This is usually in the first or last sentence.
- Look for (3) ________ (examples, statistics, etc) that show why a main idea is correct.

2 Read the text and choose the best title.

a Improving your memory
b Memories we can't forget
c Internet safety

3 Match the headings (1–4) to the correct paragraphs (A–D).

1 Freedom to be deleted
2 How the mind works
3 How the internet affects memories
4 The internet is changing us

A ____
The internet has allowed us access to much more information than many of us ever thought possible, but does it also take away something from us, making us somehow less human? Viktor Mayer-Schönberger, professor at the Oxford Internet Institute, argues that internet privacy is not so much about legal or technical arguments but a far more important issue than that.

B ____
When we remember a situation from our past we do not always remember it accurately. Unsurprisingly, we are more likely to focus on the positives than the negatives. We also rewrite the situations in our mind to make things more positive. So, the football game you played OK in is one you remember for your Messi-like performance. And that relationship you had a few years ago was perfect – you were Romeo and she was Juliet! The memories are in your mind, so you create them.

C ____
The internet, however, does not let us do this. Once you have posted, tweeted, blogged or uploaded memories, they stay there for much longer – perhaps even forever. We constantly change who we are based on our current values. Look at things you wrote when you were younger and see how much you have changed. You might be a bit embarrassed by the things you did. Your memory lets you forget these things, but digital memories remind us of our past failures, Mayer-Schönberger argues. They are often 'live' for a very long time. Over 50% of people regret something they have posted online.

D ____
Consequently, some people argue that we should have the right to be forgotten. They think internet companies have too much power and hold too much information about us and that we should be able to 'delete' our online selves completely. Do we really want high definition videos detailing exactly what we did to stay on the internet forever? Perhaps it's better to keep the memories in our minds …

4 Read the text again and choose the correct option.

1 People might want to listen to Viktor Mayer-Schönberger on this topic because …
a he studies this area and knows a lot about it.
b he is an expert on law.
2 People normally pay more attention to …
a negative memories.   b positive memories.
3 What examples of memories does the writer give? (choose two answers)
a sports success   b bad accidents
c happy family moments   d romance
4 Memories are ____ now that we have the internet.
a different   b the same
5 What do some people think about internet companies, according to the text?
a They benefit society.
b They have too much power and information.

5 Look at these sentences from the text. Match them to the correct function in the box.

example   explanation   statistic

1 Unsurprisingly, you are more likely to focus on the positives than the negatives. ________
2 And that relationship you had a few years ago was perfect – you were Romeo and she was Juliet! ________
3 Over 50% of people regret something have posted online. ________

GO BEYOND

Search online for a famous person you know. What information (photos, websites, articles) can you find about them?

____
____
____
____

Would you be happy for this much information about you to be on the internet? Why?/Why not?

GRAMMAR 1 Present perfect simple

»»» Connect past actions with the present

1 Complete the grammar table with the words and phrases in the box.

dates ever (x3) experiences never past participle periods of time recent the exact time

Present perfect simple
Form: *have/has* + (1) ....
Use A ■ For past actions when we don't know (2) .... : *Have you seen the video they made?*
Use B ■ with *ever* and *never* For (3) .... in your life: *I have (4) .... uploaded photos to the internet – not even once.* *Have you (5) .... written a blog?* Use (6) .... with a superlative adjective to emphasise how good or bad something is. *This is the worst internet connection I've (7) .... had.*
Use C ■ with *just*, *yet* and *already* For (8) .... events: *I've just finished downloading it.*
Use D ■ with *for* and *since* For actions that started in the past and continue to now: *I've been logged on for three hours.* *for* + (9) .... *since* + (10) .... , points in time

2 Read the sentences and choose which use (A–D) in the table they relate to.

1 Have you ever lost any files? A/B/C/D
2 This is the hardest test I've ever taken. A/B/C/D
3 I've eaten there five times. A/B/C/D
4 Have you finished already? A/B/C/D
5 He has never lost a game. A/B/C/D
6 They haven't finished yet. A/B/C/D
7 She hasn't posted for three days. A/B/C/D
8 She's been to Madrid. A/B/C/D

3 › Complete the sentences with the past participle forms of the verbs in brackets.

1 I've never .... (win) a game of chess against my sister Alice.
2 You've .... (break) my USB stick!
3 They've .... (catch) the person who hacked into my account.
4 Oh, no! I've .... (forget) to close down the program.
5 You've already .... (send) your application, but I haven't even .... (write) mine yet.
6 My parents have only just .... (learn) how to swipe their visa card to pay for things.
7 I've .... (ring) you three times already today.
8 I've just .... (sell) my old phone on eBay.

4 › Correct the mistakes in the conversation.

1 Don't tell me you've finished that ~~yet~~! already
2 Yes, this program is the easiest one I've ever use. ____
3 and 4 Really? I has made lots of mistakes with it. I never used one like it before. ____ ____
5 Have you ever edit photos before? ____
6 Yes, I have. But … I hasn't done it for a long time. ____
7 I've used photo-editing programs since five years now. You can soon forget how to use them though. ____
8 Well, I have forgot. I really need more practice. ____

5 › Choose the correct options to complete the conversation.

Luiza: Hi! I (1) ***haven't seen*** / ***didn't see*** you for so long. How long (2) ***was it*** / ***has it been*** ?
Antri: I'm not sure. (3) ***For*** / ***Since*** last March, I think. (4) ***I've got*** / ***I got*** photos on my phone.
Luiza: Look at the date. When was it?
Antri: Um, (5) ***it's been*** / ***it was*** early April.
Luiza: That long ago?! So what (6) ***have you done*** / ***did you do*** since then?
Antri: (7) ***I've been*** / ***I went*** to England for the summer.
Luiza: Really? Where exactly (8) ***did you go*** / ***have you been*** ?
Antri: To London!
Luiza: Come on then; let's see some pictures!

6 ›› Complete the sentences with *just*, *yet* or *already*.

1 I've ____ finished doing it this minute.
2 Haven't you finished that ____ ? Hurry up.
3 How many photos have you downloaded ____ ?
4 Give me a chance. I've only ____ switched it on!
5 The file is quite big. It hasn't uploaded ____ .
6 I've ____ done the first part. I did that the other day.
7 It's too late. She's ____ posted it online this moment.
8 Have you eaten lunch ____ ?

7 ›› Complete the advice on digital footprints with the present perfect form of the verbs in the box. Use each verb once only.

add admit finish set share tag

1 Would you lend your toothbrush to someone else? Well, your passwords are not that different to your toothbrush, so make sure you ____ them with anyone.

2 Always remember to log off when you ____ with a program.

3 Make sure you ____ your Facebook account to 'private'.

4 ____ anyone ____ you in their photos? Report or remove tags you are not happy with.

5 Remove any photos you ____ to your profile on sites such as Flickr.

6 Be careful what you post. Many employers and colleges ____ to looking at applicants' online information.

8 ››› You're helping a friend with his computer. Use the prompts to write questions using the present perfect.

1 turn on / your computer
Have you turned on your computer?
2 log on / to your computer
____
3 download / any files
____
4 back up / your files
____
5 click the icon / to update your security software
____
6 run / a security scan
____

LISTENING

››› Use the audio type, grammar and pronunciation to help you understand

1 Complete the tips with the words in the box.

REMEMBER HOW TO ...

use the audio type, grammar and pronunciation to help you understand

audio intonation stressed verbs

- Identify the type of (1) .... (a conversation, a talk, the news, etc). ☐
- Listen for (2) .... Are people talking about the past, present or future? ☐
- Listen for (3) .... words. They communicate the meaning. ☐
- Listen for big changes in (4) .... They show strong feelings. ☐

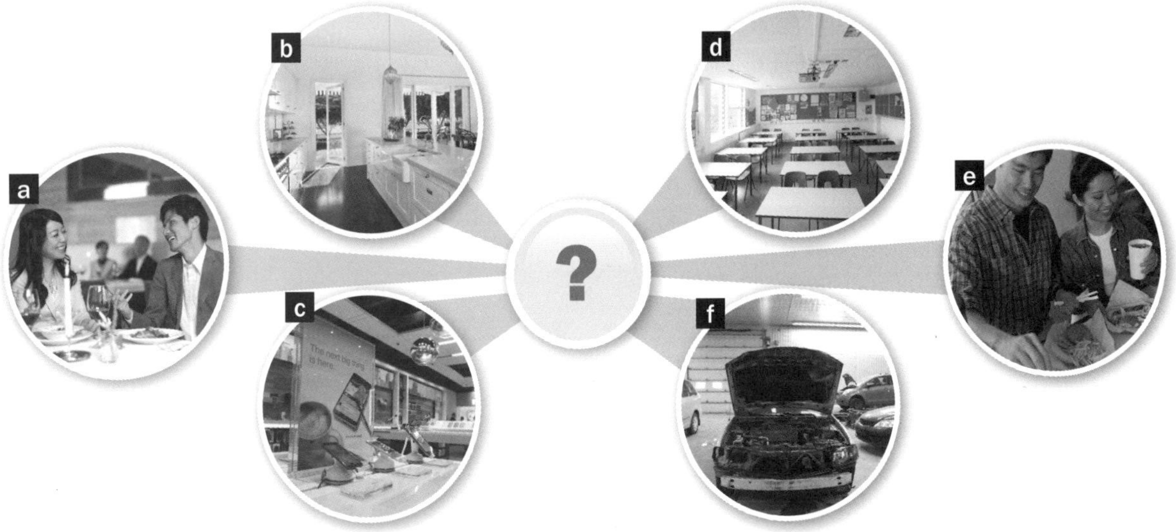

2 ▶05 Listen to three conversations. Where are the people? Write a place (a–f) next to each conversation (1–3).

a restaurant
b home
c phone shop
d school
e takeaway
f mechanic's

Conversation 1 ......
Conversation 2 ......
Conversation 3 ......

3 ▶05 Listen again. What are they talking about? Write the correct option (a–f) next to each conversation (1–3).

a using a laptop in school
b slow service
c a memory problem
d using a phone in class
e an expensive service
f a battery problem

Conversation 1 ......
Conversation 2 ......
Conversation 3 ......

4 ▶05 Listen again and decide if the statements are True (*T*) or False (*F*).

Conversation 1

1 They haven't been waiting long for their food. T/F
2 Robert is happy to post a comment. T/F

Conversation 2

3 The battery doesn't work. T/F
4 He says he's been using the product a lot. T/F

Conversation 3

5 Melanie was using the internet on her phone. T/F
6 She gets caught in class a lot. T/F

5 ▶06 Listen to the sentences from the conversations and mark the stressed word in each sentence.

1 I ordered our food thirty minutes ago.
2 I can't do that!
3 I only bought this two months ago and the battery needs replacing already.
4 You're always getting caught!
5 Yesterday in maths; the day before in chemistry and in physics.

6 Which tips in the *Remember how to* box helped you answer the questions? Tick (✓) them.

VOCABULARY 2

Negative prefixes: *un-* and *in-*

1 Correct the mistake in *italics* in each sentence.

1 Downloading some music is ~~*unlegal*~~. illegal
2 I think it's *illikely* that your computer has been infected. ________
3 You can ignore that. It's *unrelevant*. ________
4 It doesn't take that long to download. You're really *inpatient*. ________
5 I was *inaware* that the volume was turned up so high. ________
6 I think that site is *unmoral*. ________
7 It's *infair* that she gets a new phone and I don't! ________
8 This program is so *unlogical*. ________
9 My dad is *imcapable* of using this phone. ________
10 It's *unresponsible* to let young children use these sites. ________

2 a Write the correct prefix (*un*, *il*, *im*, *ir* or *in*) before each word.

1	in capable	7	____logical
2	____patient	8	____likely
3	____legal	9	____fair
4	____responsible	10	____moral
5	____relevant	11	____aware
6	____well	12	____usual

b Use the words in Exercise 2a to complete the sentences.

1 I've been feeling ________ since Monday.
2 Sorry but that argument is ________ . It doesn't make any sense.
3 This site is ________ in some countries.
4 Why would he need to know that? That's ________ , isn't it?
5 I think it's ________ that my parents limit the amount of time I'm allowed to spend online.
6 You're ________ to win. She never gets beaten.
7 He's so ________ . He expects people to be as quick at doing things as he is.
8 Sorry, I was ________ of the fact we have to update our passwords every month.
9 She wears some really ________ clothes. Have you seen these photos? She's so original.
10 I think it's ________ for parents to allow young children on social media sites.
11 It's ________ to advertise unhealthy food to young children.
12 She's ________ of staying offline for more than a few minutes.

WORDS & BEYOND

3 Choose the correct option to complete the sentences.

1 For some people it's important to remain ***anonymous*** / ***unique***, so that no-one knows who they are.
2 Some websites ***track*** / ***reveal*** the website you used before theirs and the one you use afterwards.
3 I can't ***make out*** / ***make your case*** who that is in the background.
4 I've tried to ***develop*** / ***erase*** my internet profile so that it looks more professional.
5 For me, ***privacy*** / ***issue*** is important. I don't want people knowing too much about me.
6 I didn't realise the website could ***remain*** / ***give away*** your photos to other companies.
7 There's a ***cashpoint*** / ***CCTV*** camera nearby, which caught the criminals attempting to rob the bank.
8 Google is such a well-known ***brand*** / ***advertising space*** that people actually use it as a verb.

4 Complete this paragraph with the words and phrases in the box.

getting into the wrong hands issue on the contrary out of sight tagging somebody in a photo

My internet Nightmare

Some people use the internet non-stop. They're happy to post everything and anything and don't see this as a(n) (1) ________ . They think nothing of (2) ________ even if the person is not keen. (3) ________ , they think everyone would want to be named. However, some people are more private and worry about their personal information (4) ________ . Unfortunately, once you're on the internet, it can be very difficult to remove yourself. Even if you're (5) ________ , your records are probably still backed up on Google or Facebook somewhere …

GRAMMAR 2 Present perfect continuous

»» Talk about activities in progress before or until now

1 Complete the grammar table with the words/endings in the box.

been continuous form *-ing* simple form *since*

Present perfect continuous
Use 1: With *for/* (1) ______ for actions that started in the past and continue to now.
Use 2: For actions in progress recently.
Form: *have/has* + (2) ______ + verb + (3) ______
Remember: Use the present perfect (4) ______ to emphasise how long or difficult an action was: *I've been working on this all week.*
Use the present perfect (5) ______ to emphasise the result of an action, especially to say how much or how many times: *I've emailed ten people.*
The simple and continuous forms with *for* and *since* often have a similar meaning: *I've studied English since I was seven.* *I've been studying English since I was seven.*

2 Read the following situations and tick (✓) the best tense (a or b) in each case.

1 A boy scored five goals in a football game in the first half. It's half time. He rings his dad to tell him about his performance.
   a 'I've scored five goals.' ☐
   b 'I've been scoring five goals.' ☐

2 You finished your homework ten minutes ago. Your parents said you could watch television after that. You tell them your homework is done.
   a 'I've been doing my homework.' ☐
   b 'I've done my homework.' ☐

3 A girl answers the phone. It's her mother. Her mother wants to know why she's not home from school yet. The girl's still in her science class. She started doing a special project with her teacher an hour ago. She tells her mum why she's still at school.
   a 'I've done my project.' ☐
   b 'I've been doing my project.' ☐

3 › Complete the conversations with the present perfect continuous form of the verbs in brackets.

Lisa: I (1) ______ (watch) that new series on TV. Have you?
Ciara: No, I haven't had time. I (2) ______ (work) on that IT project.

Mum: Where have you been? I (3) ______ (wait) ages for you!
Ahmed: Sorry, I (4) ______ (sit) in traffic. The roads are terrible.

Gloria: What (5) ______ you ______ (do)?
Tina: I (6) ______ (tidy) my room.

Shadia: Hi Lujain! Sorry … you (7) ______ (not stand) there long, have you?
Lujain: It's OK. Is your phone switched off? I (8) ______ (try) to call you.

4 ›› In each pair of sentences, match the sentence halves.

1 He's sent *b* — a the same message to everyone all week.
2 He's been sending *a* — b a text to his dad.

3 He's won ___ — a the game.
4 He's been winning ___ — b games all his life.

5 I've worked ___ — a in Hong Kong for the last six months.
6 I've been working ___ — b in Hong Kong.

7 I've picked up ___ — a the tickets.
8 I've been picking up ___ — b rubbish in the playground just now.

5 ››› Complete the sentences with the present perfect simple or continuous form of the verbs in the box.

finish make read send study try wait work

1 We ______ dinner. Here you go – fresh from the oven. Enjoy!
2 I ______ on it all morning and I still have more to do, but I'm really tired now.
3 How long ______ you ______ here?
4 I ______ the first 10 pages but I still have another 255 to go.
5 I ______ 50 texts so far today.
6 She ______ it yet.
7 Can you help? I ______ to do this all morning with no success.
8 He loves it. He ______ politics for two years. It's great he says.

SPEAKING

Give warnings and prohibitions

1 07 **Listen to the conversation. For each question, choose the correct option.**

1 Where are the two people?
  a in a school
  b in a computer shop
  c on a trip
2 Why is one person being told the rules/given warnings?
  a he is in trouble
  b he doesn't know about computers
  c he is new to the place

2 **Complete the *Phrasebook* with the words in the box.**

ban careful (x2) forbidden out steps take trust

3 07 **Listen again and check your answers to Exercise 2. Tick (✓) the phrases as you hear them.**

4 **Read the situations below and decide which circle to put them in. Write the number (1–5) in the correct circle.**

Giving warnings: *1*

Giving prohibitions:

1 Your friend has no virus protection on his computer.
2 Your sister wants to read your diary.
3 Your 14-year-old brother wants to drive your dad's car.
4 You're in your friend's car. He's parking, but there's a 'No Parking' sign there.
5 Your dad is using an unknown internet site.

5 08 **Listen and repeat the warnings and prohibitions. Pay attention to intonation.**

6 a **Prepare a conversation for one of the situations in Exercise 4. Include some of the phrases from the *Phrasebook* in your conversation. Look at the example for ideas.**

Example (Your friend is drinking coffee next to his computer.)
A: Are you sure that's a good idea?
B: What?
A: Drinking that next to the computer.
B: It'll be fine.
A: You know there's a ban on drinking in here, don't you?
B: Yes, yes. Don't worry.
A: Look out! Here comes Mrs Sainsbury.

....
....
....
....
....
....
....

b **Practise your conversation. Record it if you can.**

PHRASEBOOK

Giving prohibitions

You can't go/ (1) .... ☐
You're not allowed to wait/ask ...
It's prohibited/ (2) .... ☐
There's also a (3) .... on eating/walking ... ☐

Giving warnings

Watch (4) .... ! / Look out! / Be (5) .... ! ☐
Mind the (6) .... /gap. ☐
Are you sure you (7) .... that site / that's a good idea? ☐
I'd watch out / be careful if I were you.
You might download/have ... if you're not (8) .... ☐
You could fall / hurt yourself ...

WRITING

Organise information in informal emails and letters

1 Complete the expressions in the *Remember how to* box. Then say which ones are:

1 expressions used to finish emails.
2 expressions used at the beginning of emails.

REMEMBER HOW TO …

organise information in informal emails and letters

- Start with an expression like (1) *H* ___ *a* ___ *y* ___ *?* and mention your last contact. (2) *It was g* ___ *to h* ___ *f* ___ *y* ___ .
- Continue with expressions like *I'm writing to … , Apart from that, One other/last thing …*
- Use (3) *b* ___ *t* ___ *w* ___ to introduce new information.
- Use expressions like (4) *D* ___ *y* ___ *r* ___ *r … ?* to refer back to something.
- Use *Anyway, …* or *Well, …* to start saying goodbye.
- End with (5) *B* ___ *w* ___ *s* , *All the best*, etc. Use *Love* with family and close friends.

2 Read the email below and answer the questions.

1 When were Lucy and Hannah probably last in contact?
a several months ago
b several weeks ago
c earlier this week
2 Why is Hannah writing?
To get ___ ___ ___ .
3 What does she want to know about Lucy?
How the ___ for the ___ went.

Hi Lucy,

How's it going? It was great to chat on the phone the other day – I love the photos you've uploaded as well ☺.

I'm getting in touch to see if you've got Clare's contact details. I dropped my phone in the bath the other day and lost loads of my contacts. I've got some written down in messages but I've lost most of them! Could you let me know Clare's number?

By the way, did you get that Saturday job? How was the interview? I hope it went well and you're now 'rich'! What about that summer job I had? It was so boring, but at least I was able to buy lots of clothes with the money I earned …

So, hope to hear from you soon.

Take care,

Hannah

3 Read the email again and match each phrase (1–6) to its function (a–e). Use one function twice.

1 How's it going? ___	a starting expression
2 It was great to chat the other day. ___	b referring back
3 I'm getting in touch … ___	c reason for writing
4 What about … ___	d ending expression
5 So … ___	e starting to say goodbye
6 Take care, ___	

4 Complete the expressions with the words in the box.

hear (x2) know remember touch written

1 It was good to ___ from you too.
2 Sorry I haven't ___ for such a long time.
3 Just to let you ___ : this is my new email address.
4 You ___ I was writing a blog …
5 I hope to ___ from you again soon.
6 I'll be in ___ soon.

5 Find and underline six expressions in the email that are too formal. Replace them with the phrases in the box.

a I hope to hear from you again soon.
b Just to let you know
c Take care
d Sorry I haven't written for such a long time.
e You remember
~~f It was good to hear from you.~~

9:30

INBOX new reply forward next delete

Dear Una,

I was delighted to hear from you last week. 1 *f*

Please accept my apologies for not contacting you sooner. 2 ___

As you may recall I'm visiting my cousin at the moment and he hasn't got a great internet connection. It's so hard to live without it, but we've been having a lot of fun together. 3 ___

How are things with you? Has your brother come back from university yet?
For your reference, this is my new email address. 4 ___

I look forward to hearing from you soon. 5 ___

Yours sincerely, 6 ___

Aldona

WRITING PLAN

6 **You've just got back from a holiday and you're going to write an email to a friend. Your email account was hacked (accessed by someone else without permission) when you opened an email, so you need to send a warning to your friend. Use the *Writing plan* to help you prepare.**

WRITING PLAN

Make notes for your email.

Include phrases from the *Remember how to* box to start, finish and introduce information. ☐

Share some information about your holiday. ☐

Give your warning. ☐

Make comments on what your friend has been doing. ☐

Note: Look back at the warnings on page 23. Have you chosen a similar expression for your email? ☐

WRITE AND CHECK

7 **Write your email. Then tick (✓) the stages in the *Writing plan*.**

Deal with peer pressure

GET THINKING

1 **In which of these areas do you feel pressure from your peers?**

behaviour ☐ clothes ☐ hobbies ☐ music ☐ other ☐

2 **What are your peers most influenced by? Order these influences from 1–5. *1* = biggest influence and *5* = smallest influence. (There's no right answer. It's your opinion!)**

a the need to be liked ☐
b the fear that other kids will make fun of them ☐
c the wish to try something new ☐
d the idea that 'everyone is doing it' so they should too ☐
e the wish to try something dangerous ☐

3 **Read this situation. Why do you think Marek made the decision he did?**

Marek's been doing well in maths all year. He's one of the best students in class and his teachers think he should go to university to study maths. They're having a final maths quiz in class today. It doesn't count towards his mark but Marek is keen to do well. Most of his friends don't want to do it because the summer holidays are starting tomorrow. One of Marek's friends says to him, 'Come on! *All* of us are missing maths. Who can be bothered with that quiz? It's a waste of time. We're going to play football instead. Let's go!' Marek wants to fit in and thinks pleasing his friends is more important than the quiz. He decides to miss the class. When he meets with his friends, there are only two of them there. They don't have enough people for a game of football so just hang around.

4 **Think about Marek's situation and answer the questions below.**

1 What advice would you give Marek? ....

2 What are the possible consequences of his decision? ....

1 Use the picture clues to complete the crossword with words for sports.

Down 1

Across

3

4

9

10

11

12

2

5

6

7

8

2 Use the clues to complete the phrases from Unit 2.

1 When you get a new computer you need to s ___ it ___ p.
2 You like a photo on an internet site, so you decide to d ___ d it.
3 People like to u ___ d photos to websites to share them with friends.
4 You usually need to l ___ n before you can use a computer.
5 To stop people accessing your email you must remember to l ___ t.
6 I s ___ e my card to pay for things.
7 If you can't hear it, then t ___ it ___ p.
8 Save energy. T ___ things ___ f when you're not using them.
9 You need to t ___ it ___ n before you can use it.
10 It's too loud! T ___ it ___ n, please.

3 Match each situation to the best word in the box.

illegal illogical impatient incapable irresponsible unaware unfair ~~unlikely~~ unusual unwell

1 You win a million pounds. *unlikely*
2 They forget to collect their child from school. ___
3 It wasn't her fault and she knows this, but she feels totally responsible. ___
4 A millionaire wins the lottery. ___
5 An employee steals from a shop. ___
6 I just can't remember my password. I've tried too many times now. ___
7 She's normally here by nine. ___
8 I just hate waiting! ___
9 I didn't know this site existed. ___
10 I feel terrible! ___

ALL ABOUT ME

1 Are any internet activities more risky than extreme sports?

___

2 Name something that:

- **makes you impatient.** ___
- **you were unaware of last week.** ___
- **you think is unfair.** ___
- **you think you're incapable of doing.** ___

1 Complete the conversation with the correct form of the verbs in brackets. Use the past continuous, past simple or present perfect continuous.

Ana: I rang you at 12 o'clock but you (1) ________ (not / answer) your phone.
Octavio: Sorry, I (2) ________ (travel) on the metro and couldn't hear it.
Ana: Are you OK?
Octavio: I'm a bit tired. I (3) ________ (travel) all day.
Ana: Why?
Octavio: I (4) ________ (visit) Paola this morning. Then, when I (5) ________ (come) home on the train, it (6) ________ (break) down.
Ana: Oh, no! What did you do?
Octavio: I (7) ________ (take) every type of transport you can imagine – first a bus, then a taxi … bike … train. I didn't really know what I was doing. I never want to go through that again.
Ana: You should get this travel app. I (8) ________ (use) it for a few months now, and it's great.
Octavio: How much (9) ________ (you / pay) for it?
Ana: Nothing. It's free.
Octavio: Why (10) ________ (you / tell) me before!

2 Complete the conversation with the correct options (a, b, c or d).

Antri: Hi Abdul. I (1) ___ seen you for a long time.
Abdul: Hi Antri. Great to see you. What have you (2) ___ doing?
Antri: (3) ___ just been on holiday.
Abdul: Where did you go?
Antri: We (4) ___ to Croatia. Have you (5) ___ there?
Abdul: No, I haven't.
Antri: Something really surprising happened on holiday. We (6) ___ next to the pool when Eve walked past!
Abdul: What was she (7) ___ there?
Antri: Her family (8) ___ on a cruise and the boat stopped in Dubrovnik for the night.
Abdul: Very strange!

	a	b	c	d
1	a didn't	b hasn't	c wasn't	d haven't
2	a was	b is	c been	d had
3	a I'll	b I've	c I'd	d I'm
4	a went	b go	c have gone	d are going
5	a did	b been	c was	d went
6	a sat	b have been sitting	c were sitting	d had sat
7	a did	b do	c done	d doing
8	a travelled	b travel	c were travelling	d have travelled

3 Complete the second sentence so that it has a similar meaning to the first. Use three to five words including the word in brackets.

1 She had her phone in her hand.
(holding) She *was holding her* phone.
2 In the middle of the night there was a knock on the door.
(sleeping) I ________ there was a knock on the door.
3 This phone has been mine for two years.
(had) I ________ phone for two years.
4 He doesn't have his phone.
(got) He ________ .
5 I stopped playing tennis two minutes ago and I'm tired.
(been) I've just ________ and I'm tired.
6 My wait on the phone has lasted 30 minutes so far.
(waited) I ________ on the phone for 30 minutes.

4 Complete the sentences with the verbs in the box. Use the present simple or the present simple passive.

be need not think strap travel use (x2)

1 A rope ________ in bungee jumping but one ________ in base jumping.
2 You ________ strong winds for windsurfing.
3 I ________ tower running is a sport. It sounds like hard work to me!
4 Body surfing ________ like body boarding without the board.
5 When you learn to skydive, you ________ to an instructor.
6 Free divers ________ to great depths – way below the surface of the water.

3 EYEWITNESS

UNIT

VOCABULARY 1 >>> Talk about natural disasters in films

1 Label the natural features.

1 h..........

2 m..........

3 b..........

4 f..........

5 f..........

6 v..........

7 c..........

8 l..........

9 r..........

10 w..........

11 w..........

12 i..........

2 a First use the clues to write the words (1–9). Then check your answers by finding them in the word search.

1 l ... ... a — melted rock
2 f ... ... d — a lot of water that covers a usually dry area
3 w ... ... e — a fire that starts in the countryside and spreads quickly
4 d ... ... t — a long period without rain
5 t ... ... o — a strong wind that goes round in circles over land
6 t ... ... i — a large wave
7 d ... ... h — the end of life
8 s ... ... — strong wind and heavy rain
9 r ... ... — water that falls from the sky

P	E	D	E	A	T	H	S	V	H
W	R	Z	C	O	H	M	O	P	G
L	I	D	R	O	U	G	H	T	T
A	F	N	Q	H	E	S	I	O	F
V	D	I	I	V	T	X	R	L	K
A	L	A	H	O	J	N	O	D	L
L	I	R	R	P	A	O	X	A	M
N	W	M	J	D	D	K	R	C	L
J	Y	Y	O	S	H	K	A	H	Z
T	S	U	N	A	M	I	W	A	V

b Find one more word in the word search that's a disaster caused by people.

w ... ...

3 Complete the sentences with the words in the box.

death drought flood lava storm tornado tsunami wildfire

1 There was no rain for months, causing a very serious ...., which destroyed crops and cost the lives of many farm and wild animals.
2 The volcano erupted with a loud bang, and huge amounts of ash and .... were sent up into the air blocking out the sun.
3 The whole forest seems to be burning as the .... spreads.
4 There has so far been one .... and several serious injuries caused by the bad weather.
5 With its extremely strong winds, a .... can lift almost anything from the ground.
6 The height of the .... was about 50 metres when it reached the coast.
7 A violent .... with heavy rainfall has led to a dangerous rise in the river level.
8 Photographs show large areas of farmland under water as the .... spreads.

4 Match the sentences (1–6) to the disasters (a–f).

1 ..... *We closed everything and made sure the dogs were inside when we saw it coming straight towards our house.*

2 ..... *We were skiing down the mountain when we heard a loud noise behind us. We just managed to get out of the way in time.*

3 ..... *I woke up and everything was shaking. Things were falling off shelves, and windows were breaking – there was glass everywhere.*

4 ..... *After days of heavy rain, suddenly tons of mud and rocks started to flow down the hill – it was terrifying.*

5 ..... *It was frightening being in a small boat miles from land in such weather. I don't know how we survived such strong winds, high waves and heavy rain.*

6 ..... *Golden rivers of melted rock were moving towards us from the summit. It was time to get out of there.*

a earthquake
b landslide
c volcanic eruption
d avalanche
e hurricane
f tornado

Recognise and understand similes

1 Complete the tips with the words in the box.

REMEMBER HOW TO …

recognise and understand similes

compare comparisons picture qualities

1 Look for sentences which ____________ two things or people.
2 Look for ____________ with *as* … *as*, *like* … and (*looked*/*felt*/*sounded*) *as if* … .
3 Think about what ____________ the two things share. Try and build a ____________ in your mind.

2 Read the extract below from a newspaper article. How many countries are mentioned?

____

EXTREME WEATHER: *Typhoons and Twisters*

The power of the wind is one of the strongest and most destructive forces on the planet, causing physical damage, human suffering and loss of life. The year 2013 saw two record-breaking examples of the wind's terrible force. First, a tornado (or twister) hit Oklahoma in the United States in June. Then, monster storm Super Typhoon Usagi – over 1,100 kilometres from one side to the other – struck Taiwan and surrounding countries in September. We have eyewitness reports from people who were caught up in both events.

Ben from Oklahoma, USA: This was truly an experience. We're used to twisters in these parts, but this thing was over four kilometres wide and the winds it created blew at incredible speeds of up to 480 kilometres an hour. It was like a giant smashing its way across the land picking up and throwing away anything in its path. Cars were thrown around as easily as an angry kid throws a toy against a wall. You couldn't do anything to stop its progress!

Li from Taiwan: A typhoon is a strong tropical storm and this one was categorised as a Super Typhoon, which is similar to a Category 5 hurricane. It was actually – at the time – the most powerful storm there'd been on Earth for nearly 30 years. We knew it was coming, so we'd prepared as well as we could. There was so much wind and rain beating on the roof that even in the house it sounded like you'd got the vacuum cleaner on and you'd got your ear right next to it!

3 Read the text again and underline three similes.

4 Look at the similes in bold *italics*. Can you guess what they mean? Choose a or b.

1 My bag feels ***as light as a feather*** without my school books in it.
2 That test was ***as easy as falling off a log*** – I think I got a good score for once!
3 CJ might look stupid but, believe me, he's ***as clever as a fox***.
4 That story's ***as old as the hills***. I think my great-grandad told me it.
5 Wow! That Usain Bolt sure is ***as quick as lightning*** – look at him run.
6 Katy, what a lovely dress! You look ***as pretty as a picture***.

1	a	very heavy	b	not heavy at all
2	a	difficult	b	not difficult at all
3	a	intelligent	b	not intelligent
4	a	modern/new	b	not new at all
5	a	very fast	b	not fast at all
6	a	very nice	b	not nice at all

5 Complete the similes with your own words.

1 Your bedroom looks like *a bomb has hit it*.
2 Everyone was running around like ____________.
3 You're as silly as a ____________.
4 The survivors were as thin as ____________.

GO BEYOND

Use the internet to find an article in English about a natural disaster that happened in your country. Find a **good news story** that happened after it, eg about someone being rescued. Did you find any similes in the article? Write them below: ____________

GRAMMAR 1 Past perfect simple and past perfect continuous

Talk about actions before another time in the past

1 Complete the grammar table with the words and phrases in the box.

finished in progress past participle realise since state verb yet

Past perfect simple
Use: For an action that (1) ________ before another past action or time. **Form:** *had/hadn't* + (2) ________
Past perfect continuous
Use: For an action (3) ________ up to a time in the past. **Form:** *had/hadn't* + (4) ________ + *-ing*
Words often used with the past perfect simple: *after, before, just* and (5) ________ .
Verbs that are not usually used with the past perfect continuous: (6) ________ verbs such as *understand, know* and (7) ________ .
You can use both forms with *for* and (8) ________ .
Note 1: You don't need to use the past perfect when it's clear which of two actions happened first or when the two actions happened very close together. Then we can put both verbs in the past simple. *I turned off the light and went to sleep.* *She stopped and listened carefully.* **Note 2:** Sometimes either form can be used without much difference in meaning. *She'd* ***been working/worked*** *there for 30 years and decided it was time to stop.*

2 › Choose the correct sentence in each pair.

1 a I hadn't heard about that book until you mentioned it.
  b I hadn't been hearing about that book until you mentioned it.
2 a She hadn't been realising before just how beautiful the view was.
  b She hadn't realised before just how beautiful the view was.
3 a He knew that he'd been here before.
  b He'd been knowing that he was here before.
4 a I tried to contact him for ages, but he'd never replied.
  b I'd been trying to contact him for ages, but he never replied.
5 a She didn't see him since they had been at school.
  b She hadn't seen him since they were at school.
6 a I already survived one disaster so I'd been prepared for this latest one.
  b I'd already survived one disaster so I was prepared for this latest one.

3 › Match the sentence halves.

1 She hadn't decided yet which
2 They'd been sweating for hours
3 He realised that he'd made
4 I hadn't been expecting the climb
5 They'd been looking for survivors
6 Finally, I'd saved enough money
7 We'd been waiting since
8 Fortunately he'd already crossed

a under the hot sun.
b trip to go on.
c but with no success.
d the bridge.
e for the operation.
f a terrible mistake.
g early morning.
h to be so hard.

4 » Choose the correct options to complete the text.

I was quite surprised to find out that my grandfather had never actually (1) ***met*** / ***been meeting*** my grandmother – not even once – before they arranged to get married. Charles had been fighting in India in the army and Lillian had (2) ***known*** / ***been knowing*** his brother, Steve, back in England. She'd (3) ***been seeing*** / ***seen*** a photo of Charles, and Steve suggested that she could write to him in India as he hadn't (4) ***got*** / ***been getting*** a single letter in months. He'd (5) ***been waiting*** / ***waited*** for some communication from home and was amazed when he was told that a letter had finally (6) ***been arriving*** / ***arrived***. From the dystopia of war began the utopia of love.

5 » Rearrange the words to make sentences.

1 John / understood / started out / he / dangers / the / hadn't / before / .

....

....

2 never / attempted / He'd / to / alone / climb / he felt confident / but / .

....

....

3 expected / was / told / had / him / Nobody / that / a violent storm / .

....

....

4 holding / hadn't / been / He / rope / when / the / his partner fell / .

....

....

5 He / twisted / he'd / ankle / his / thought / in the fall / .

....

....

6 arrived / He'd / when / given up / almost / the rescue team / hope / .

....

....

6 »» Complete the story with the past perfect simple or past perfect continuous form of the verbs in brackets.

I (1) *had already been planning* (already / plan) to go there with my kids, but, at the last moment, my neighbour Tilly said she wanted to come too. I didn't know this until she told me, but she (2) .... (never / be) to the safari park before – very strange considering we (3) .... (always / live) so close to it. She (4) .... (always / dream) of going when she was younger, but her parents (5) .... (say) no every single time she (6) .... (ask) them if she could go. Apparently, they (7) .... (have) a very bad experience at the safari park a long time ago.

They (8) .... (drive) through the monkey area when they suddenly heard a screech from the back seat of the car. Tilly's dad (9) .... (leave) the window open by mistake and there was a little monkey in the back chewing the leather seats of their brand new Mercedes. It (10) .... (chew) the seats for ages before either of them noticed. By that time, the inside of the car had been destroyed. Tilly's mum (11) .... (eat) a sandwich in the car just before she saw the monkey. The monkey saw the rest of the sandwich on her lap and grabbed it while making his escape out the window. Tilly's mum and dad (12) .... (have) their new car destroyed and their lunch stolen. From that day on, they hated the safari park – especially those cheeky little monkeys!

Tilly, aged 34, was the biggest kid in my car when we arrived that day – she was really excited. But, before we got there, I (13) .... (ask) everyone to make sure all the windows were up. Well, you know, just in case ...

LISTENING

Focus on important information

1 a Match the words (1–5) to the phrases (a–e) to complete the tips in the *Remember how to* box.

1 Identify	a small details and examples.
2 Focus	b people's exact words when you quote them.
3 Write	c the main topic.
4 Ignore	d only on information that relates to the main topic.
5 Listen	e for information which is repeated or emphasised.

b Now rewrite the completed tips from Exercise 1a. Try to put them in the same order as they appear in the Student's Book.

REMEMBER HOW TO …

focus on important information

1 *Identify* ……………………
2 ……………………
3 ……………………
4 ……………………
5 ……………………

2 a 09 Listen to the first part of a speech from a film. How many disasters does the speaker mention?

……………………

b Which disaster does he say affects the most people?

……………………

3 09 Listen again and note down three examples he gives of the effects of the disaster.

1 People …………………… .
2 People …………………… .
3 People …………………… .

4 Which of the three examples in Exercise 3 does he emphasise (say is particularly important or worth paying attention to)?

……………………

5 10 Listen to the second part of the speech and fill in the information.

1 Problem: ……………………
2 Important fact: ……………………

6 a 11 Listen to the third part of the speech. What's the most important piece of information, a, b or c?

a The speaker can paint houses.
b There aren't many jobs.
c The speaker has a plan to help people share their skills.

b What do the letters S.W.Y.G. stand for?

S…………… W…………… Y……………'…… G……………

7 What do you think is the most important or interesting piece of information you hear? Remember to quote exactly what the person says. (There is no right answer – it's your opinion!)

……………………
……………………
……………………

VOCABULARY 2

Noise verbs

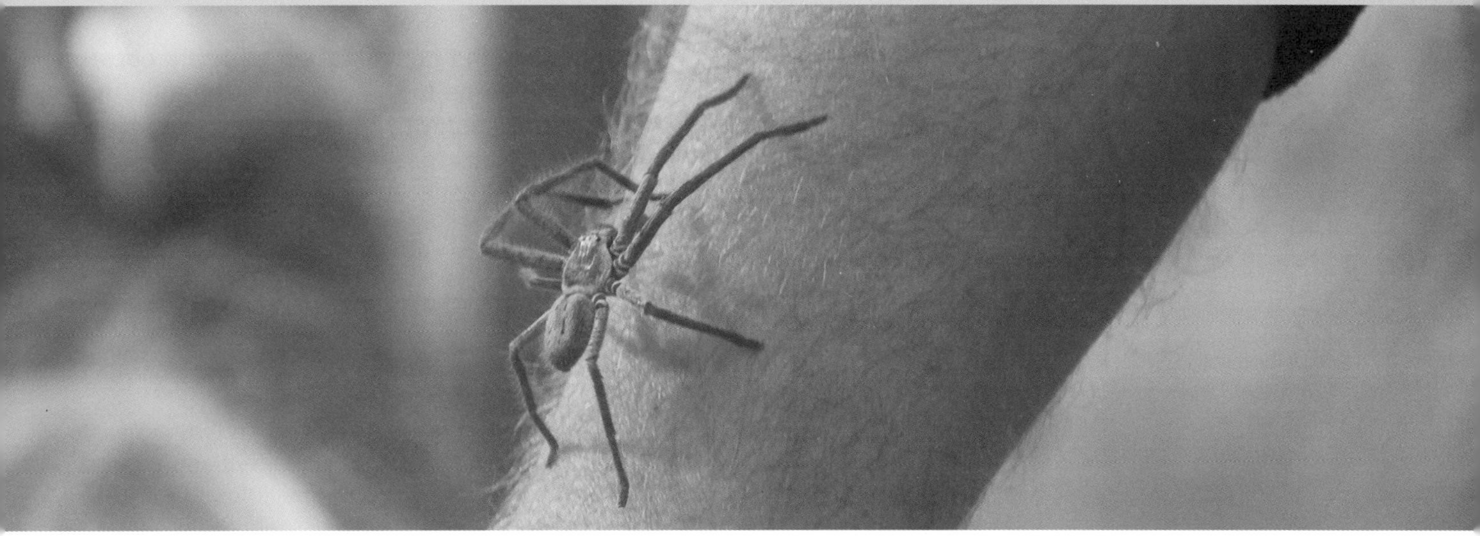

1 Match the sentence halves.

1 He screamed
2 He yelled
3 She groaned
4 The pilot crashed
5 She slammed
6 She exploded

a in a loud deep voice to be heard above the noise of the crowd.
b her hand against the table in anger.
c when he saw the giant spider on his arm.
d the bomb as planned once everyone had moved to a safe distance away.
e the plane, but luckily everyone survived.
f in pain as she was lifted into the rescue helicopter.

2 Choose the correct option to complete the sentences.

1 The open door was ***bursting*** / ***banging*** in the wind.
2 She ***sighed*** / ***groaned*** with relief when she found her car keys.
3 There was a loud 'pop' as the balloon ***exploded*** / ***burst*** .
4 I love listening to the ***yell*** / ***roar*** of the waves.
5 He ran out of the room ***slamming*** / ***exploding*** the door behind him.
6 She ***screamed*** / ***whispered*** her secret into his ear.

WORDS & BEYOND

3 Complete the text with the words in the box.

community disease global grab ignore utopia

The small (1) .... had been living happily on their island until (2) .... warming made the sea level rise and what they felt was their (3) .... , their ideal way of life, was destroyed. When it happened, it happened so suddenly that within days the island had disappeared. It's easy for us to (4) .... the problems of a small distant island, but just imagine if your family had been living without war or (5) .... for hundreds of years and you had to move through no fault of your own. What would you do? You'd have no choice but to (6) .... your possessions and try to make a new life in a new world … somehow.

4 Complete the sentences with the correct form of the verbs in the box.

creep knock snap step swing twist

1 Don't .... up on me like that – you scared me.
2 The rope suddenly .... and we began falling through the air.
3 She realised that she had .... her ankle.
4 He .... on the castle door, but there was no answer.
5 She .... onto the bridge.
6 It was going from side to side – it was .... in the wind.

GRAMMAR 2 Sense verbs + *-ing* or infinitive

››› Talk about things that you see, hear, feel and smell

1 Complete the grammar table with the words and phrases in the box.

completed   infinitive   in progress   object   smell

Sense verbs + *-ing* or infinitive
Use: To talk about actions we see, hear, feel and (1) ________ .
Form: For actions (2) ________ , use: *see/hear/feel/smell* + (3) ________ + verb + *-ing* For (4) ________ actions, use: *see/hear/feel/smell* + object + (5) ________ without *to*

2 › Complete the text with the correct verbs in the box.

coming   go off   increasing   jump
ringing   running   screaming

I didn't hear when the fire alarm started to (1) ________ because I had my headphones on, but then I smelled the smoke (2) ________ under the door and I realised something was wrong. I took off my headphones and heard the alarm (3) ________ . I couldn't see much because of the smoke, which had now filled my room. I felt the heat (4) ________ and opened the window. Below I saw people (5) ________ out of the building and heard them (6) ________ . I saw someone (7) ________ from a window above me, but because I am a Superhero I flew out and saved him.

3 ›› Complete the conversation with the correct form of the verbs in the box. Use the infinitive or *-ing* form. Look at the key before you start.

climb   cook
cry   fly   put
sing   touch

Key: ✓ = a completed action
→ = an action in progress

Hasina: Listen. Can you hear the birds (1) → ________ ?

Nazeen: What birds are they? I can't see any (2) → ________ around, can you?

Hasina: I don't think birds sing when they're flying. Oh! What was that? I just felt something (3) ✓ ________ my neck for a moment.

Nazeen: Don't worry. It was just a butterfly. There it goes. Hey. Do you see that cat (4) → ________ the tree over there?

Hasina: Yeah. It did the same thing a few nights ago. We heard it (5) → ________ because it had got stuck and couldn't get down. Silly animal! Dad had to rescue it. Right. Time to go in – I smell something (6) → ________ . I saw Mum (7) ✓ ________ a pie in the oven an hour ago. It must be ready now.

4 a ››› Rearrange the words to make sentences.

a I / of the door / from / coming / smelled / the other side / strange / something / .

____ ________________________________

b I / downstairs / something like / a window / suddenly / heard / smash / .

____ ________________________________

c I / cold sweat / in the blackness / as I stood / felt / running down my back / .

____ ________________________________

d I / alone at night / in my bedroom / go out / when / saw / was / I / the lights / .

1 ________________________________

e I / towards / my room / walking slowly / heard / up the stairs / somebody / .

____ ________________________________

f I / somebody / and repeatedly / on my door / heard / knocking loudly / .

____ ________________________________

b Now put the sentences in Exercise 4a in the correct order to make a story. The first one has been done for you.
What do you think happened next? Look at the box below to find out.

'It's Dad – open up. I was just trying to scare you by knocking like that! I've just got back. There's been a power cut. I broke some glasses in the kitchen, but I've got some takeaway food.'

Contradict facts and opinions

1 a ▶12 Complete the sentences with one word in each gap. Then listen and check your answers.

1 Well, as a ______ of fact this has been the hottest summer ever.
2 I take your ______ , but that's not due to global warming.
3 You're ______ there. The Earth's getting warmer each year.
4 I'm not ______ how true that is, actually. Last winter was also the coldest in years.
5 That's ______ , but climate change means the weather gets more extreme.
6 I don't ______ so. The planet can't be getting both hotter and colder.
7 Well, ______ it is.
8 That's not true at ______ . It doesn't make any sense.
9 The point is that it's very ______ that this extreme temperature change is just natural.
10 I'm afraid that's not ______ true. The Earth just goes through natural periods of warming and cooling – it's not our fault.

b Complete the *Phrasebook* with words from Exercise 1a.

PHRASEBOOK

- You're (1) ______ there. ☐
- I'm afraid that's not (2) ______ true. ☐
- I take your (3) ______ , but … ☐
- Well, as a (4) ______ of fact … ☐
- I'm not (5) ______ how true that is, (6) ______ . ☐
- That's not true at (7) ______ . ☐
- That's (8) ______ , but … ☐
- It's very (9) ______ . ☐
- I don't (10) ______ so. ☐

2 a ▶13 Listen to the conversation and tick (✓) the phrases from the *Phrasebook* that you hear.

b ▶14 Listen and repeat the phrases.

3 Match the statements (1–6) to the contradictions (a–f).

1 An octopus is a fish. ____
2 An elephant can jump. ____
3 A mouse has the same number of bones in its neck as a giraffe. ____
4 A cat has four legs and a tail. A dog has four legs and a tail. Therefore a dog is a cat. ____
5 A brown hen lays brown eggs. A white hen lays white eggs. ____
6 A human does not live a better life than other animals. ____

a I take your point, but surely we avoid diseases because of the medicines we have.
b I'm afraid that's not quite true. I live on a farm, so I should know.
c I don't think so. It has legs.
d It's very unlikely. Just look at the difference in size.
e You're wrong there. It's much too big and heavy.
f That's not true at all. I'm not a monkey because I have two arms and two legs.

GO BEYOND

'A gorilla is a type of monkey.'
Do some research to find out if this statement is true or false. If it's false, explain why.

______
______
______
______

WRITING

Link ideas in a story

1 Complete the tips with the words in the box.

REMEMBER HOW TO …

link ideas in a story

afterwards before finally luckily meanwhile
suddenly unfortunately when while

(1) Use words like ______, ______, ______, ______, ______ and ______ to show the order of events.
(2) Use words like ______ to say if something happened quickly or unexpectedly.
(3) Use words like ______ and ______ to show your attitude.

2 Match 1–7 to a–g to make linking phrases.

1 strangely	a as
2 as soon	b once
3 in the	c surprise
4 to my	d end
5 all at	e the blue
6 in	f enough
7 out of	g the meantime

3 Choose the correct option to complete the sentences.

1 I knew we were meant to be together ___ I saw her.
a while b as soon as c in the end
2 ___ , we'd never met before, although we had gone to the same university.
a Strangely enough b All at once c Meanwhile
3 It happened ___ – without any warning. Everyone was shocked.
a as soon as b in the end c out of the blue
4 I thought the first evening went well, but ___ she told me it had been a disaster.
a beforehand b in the meantime c afterwards
5 I fell asleep ___ dinner – it was very embarrassing.
a during b while c when
6 ___ , she wants to see me again. I thought the date was a disaster!
a All at once b Finally c To my surprise

4 Choose the correct options to complete the story.

People had been talking about the wise* man who lived on the top of a mountain and I decided to make the long and difficult journey to visit him.
(1) *Meanwhile / When* I arrived at the house, an old servant* met me at the door. 'I would like to see the wise man', I said to the servant.
He smiled and led me inside. (2) *While / During* we were walking through the house, he told me a bit about his life.
(3) *Finally, / Out of the blue*, we reached the back door. (4) *Afterwards, / To my disappointment*, nobody else was in the house. 'But I haven't met the wise man,' I said. He turned to me, looked me in the eye and (5) *beforehand / to my surprise* said, 'Perhaps you have. With everyone you meet in life – even if they appear unimportant – see each of them as a wise person. They all have something you can learn from'.

Glossary
***wise** = able to make good judgements based on deep understanding or experience of life
***servant** = a person who has a job working in another person's house

5 Choose the best title for the story.

a The older, the better b Look, listen and learn c A wasted journey

WRITING PLAN

6 You're going to write a story with one of the titles in Exercise 5. Choose the title for your story. Use the *Writing plan* to help you prepare.

WRITING PLAN

Make notes for your story.

1 Set the scene. ☐

2 Say what happened first. ☐

3 Develop the story: say what happened next. ☐

4 Add an ending: say how the story finished. ☐

And remember to:

- use a variety of tenses, eg past simple and past continuous. ☐
- link the ideas in your story, eg *At first, Then, Suddenly, In the end,* etc. ☐

WRITE AND CHECK

7 Write your story. Then tick (✓) the stages in the *Writing plan*.

Understand another person's feelings

1 Read what Kim says and tick (✓) the best two responses.

I find it really hard to meet new people. I'm scared that I'll have nothing to say and they won't like me.

1 *Yeah. Well, you can't change your personality. Not everyone can be as confident as me. Live with it.* ☐

2 *Don't be silly. There must be someone out there who'll like you.* ☐

3 *Well, try it now. Go over to that person at the bus stop and start a conversation.* ☐

4 *I totally understand what you mean. It's difficult sometimes when you're in a new social situation.* ☐

5 *You get on with your family. Isn't that enough?* ☐

6 *I'm sure we all feel like that sometimes, but think of how many friends you already have who love you.* ☐

2 a Put the advice to give Kim in order from best (1) to worst (6). (There are no right answers. Decide what you think is best.)

a Change your hairstyle. ☐
b Go out with friends to a café. ☐
c Go to cafés alone. ☐
d Take your dog for walks in the park. ☐
e Go to the cinema by yourself. ☐
f Join a gym. ☐

b Match the sentences (1–6) to the advice in Exercise 2a (a–f).

1 Then sit down at a table with people you don't know and force yourself to talk to them. ____
2 You can talk to the people you sit next to. ____
3 You'll meet lots of people who want to stop and pet it. ____
4 You might feel safer with your friends there, and they can help you meet new people. ____
5 If you look good, you'll feel good too. ____
6 You'll get to exercise and meet people at the same time. ____

c Add one more piece of advice of your own.

I think you should … because …

____

____

1 Complete the sentences with the words in the box.

back up   erase   log on   reveal   scan   unique

1 Be careful you don't ______ what you've written so you can't find it again.
2 This is your ______ password. Use it with your username to log on.
3 Don't ______ your PIN to anybody.
4 Remember to ______ all your files in case your computer crashes.
5 You can ______ any document using your printer to save and send it to your computer.
6 You need to ______ as a user before you can access some sites.

2 Choose the correct options to complete the text.

It's clearly (1) ____ to steal, but imagine there had been a disaster, such as a nuclear (2) ____ and you were one of the few (3) ____ . If you're hungry, is it wrong to (4) ____ food from a shop whose windows have all been (5) ____ in? In such a situation you have to do anything you can to (6) ____ alive and help the people around you.

	a	b	c	d
1	a incapable	b illegal	c illogical	d irrelevant
2	a warming	b bang	c eruption	d explosion
3	a survivors	b homeless	c issues	d buried
4	a crash	b click	c update	d grab
5	a smashed	b scanned	c risked	d slammed
6	a give away	b remain	c swipe	d land

3 Choose the correct option to complete the sentences.

1 Mind the ***hurt*** / ***gap*** . You're going to hurt yourself if you're not careful!
2 Watch ***out*** / ***careful*** ! You almost walked in front of that car!
3 I take your ***point*** / ***fact*** , but I still think we need a new government.
4 In point of ***truth*** / ***fact*** , I'm not late. You arrived way too early as usual.
5 On the ***opposite*** / ***contrary*** , I think she's rude and unpleasant.
6 I'm ***scared*** / ***afraid*** that's not quite true (though many people believe it is).
7 Cycling on these paths is ***forbidden*** / ***warned*** . Use the cycle track instead.
8 Using a mobile phone is ***anonymous*** / ***prohibited*** in the building. You can do what you want outside, though.

ALL ABOUT ME

1 What do you use the internet for mostly?

______

______

2 Is it fair to download music from the internet without paying for it? Why?/Why not?

______

______

3 How would you feel if you were in a place with no internet access or mobile phone signal for 48 hours?

______

______

1 Choose the correct option to complete the sentences.

You've (1) ***wrote / been writing / written*** enough operas for one day Wolfgang. Go out and (2) ***playing / play / played*** basketball with the other kids.

I (3) ***'m thinking / have thought / think*** I've just (4) ***been twisting / twisted / twist*** my ankle. I (5) ***was skateboarding / have skateboarded / skateboard*** and I (6) ***have fallen / fell / was falling*** off.

I (7) ***told / 'm telling / was told*** that a virus (8) ***was infected / had infected / will infect*** my laptop, but the repairman promised he could help.

2 Rewrite the sentences, correcting the mistakes in *italics* in each one.

1 Did John *finished to write* his report on time?
Did John finish writing his report on time?

2 *Has* the students *been heard* about the fire drill?
....

3 Do we all *knowing* what *to be done* in case of an earthquake?
....

4 After he'd *been phoning* her three times, he *was given up*.
....

5 She suddenly *was seeing* the huge wave *had come* towards her.
....

6 Where have you *been being*? *I've waited* for ages.
....

3 a Choose the correct option to complete the responses.

1 Yes, I'm afraid it ..... .
a did b doing c do

2 I hadn't known it ..... going to happen.
a had b was c been

3 That's what the weather forecast ..... .
a makes b says c has

4 I've just ..... a new course, actually.
a been b going c started

5 Well, I certainly ..... hoped to do better.
a had b did c was

6 No. Tell me what's ..... going on.
a being b was c been

b Match the responses (1–6) in Exercise 3a to the questions (a–f) below.

a What have you been doing recently? .....
b Have you heard the news? .....
c Did it break down again? .....
d Were you surprised at your results? .....
e Are they expecting more floods? .....
f Why hadn't you done anything? .....

UNIT 4 THINKING AHEAD!

VOCABULARY 1 >>> Talk about jobs and apprenticeships

1 a Rearrange the letters to form different job categories. (Look at the clues below if you need help.)

1 UACGUETLRIR
2 RTSA
3 BISSEUSN
4 CITTUSNCNORO
5 TEHHAL
6 VELATR NAD OIMUTRS
7 LEIATR

Clues

1 Farmers work in this area.
2 People who are good at painting work in this area.
3 Accountants work in this area.
4 Builders and architects work in this area.
5 Doctors and nurses work in this area.
6 Tour guides work in this area.
7 Shop assistants work in this area.

b Use the letters in the circles ◯ to form a noun that describes the period of time someone works to learn their skills.

_ P P _ _ _ _ _ _ _ _ _ _ P

2 Complete the job categories with the words in Exercise 1a.

- (1) ...., Manufacturing and Services
- (2) ...., Media and Publishing
- (3) ...., Gardening and Animal Care
- (4) ...., Education and Public Services
- (5) ....
- Information and Communication Technology
- Leisure, (6) ....
- (7) ...., Administration and Law

3 Look at the photos and complete the name of each job.

1 a _ _ ou _ _ nt
2 app/software/ _ _ _ developer
3 b _ _ _ _ y th _ _ _ ist
4 ca _ _ _ _ ter
5 el _ _ _ _ _ cian
6 fir _ _ _ _ _ ter
7 flight _ _ _ _ _ _ ant
8 _ _ _ _ ener
9 hea _ _ _ _ are assist _ _ _
10 lighting/s _ _ _ _ technician
11 plu _ _ _ _
12 _ _ _ _ _ _ _ nary nurse

4 Complete the sentences with the words in the box.

architect   estate agent   florist   lawyer   park ranger

1 *My family owns a flower shop, so when I leave school I'll probably become a(n) ....*

2 *I really enjoy design. It's my dream to become a(n) ....*

3 *I think I'd make a good salesman, so I might become a(n) ....*

4 *I'm going to study law in Manchester. In a few years hopefully I'll be a(n) ....*

5 *I love working outside. I'm not sure what job I want yet but maybe I'll be a(n) ....*

READING

Recognise formal and informal writing

1 Complete the tips with the words in the box.

REMEMBER HOW TO …

recognise formal and informal writing

complex   emoticons   greetings   punctuation   simpler

Formal writing: look for …

- formal (1) ______ and vocabulary (*Dear Mr/Ms …*).
- longer, more (2) ______ sentences with full verbs.
- correct spelling and (3) ______ .

Informal writing: look for …

- informal greetings and vocabulary (*Hi Dad*).
- shorter, (4) ______ sentences with contractions (*I'll, I don't*).
- abbreviations, exclamation marks and (5) ______ .

2 Read the text below quickly. Choose the correct topic.

a Writing CVs
b Completing an application form
c Job interviews

DO YOUR RESEARCH. Read the job description carefully. Look at the company's website and learn about what it does. This will help you learn how your knowledge and skills can benefit the company.

ARRIVE ON TIME. Practise travelling to the interview venue a few times beforehand so you know the route. On the day, try to arrive about 15 minutes before the interview starts.

DRESS APPROPRIATELY. What to wear depends on the industry and company, but always be clean and smart.

EMPHASISE ALL YOUR STRENGTHS. Lots of people with similar experience and qualifications will apply for the same job. Do not just highlight your educational background. Focus on your personal strengths too. Are you good at communicating? Are you hardworking? Let your interviewer know.

ASK QUESTIONS. This gives you a chance to check anything you are unsure of and it also shows you are interested in the job.

COMMENTS

Also, don't lie. You'll get found out! lol☺ **Lenny** *I/F*

It is very important that you are fully prepared for the interview and that means even preparing the questions you wish to ask. If you have not given consideration to the questions before the interview, it can make this stage much more challenging. **Ruby** *I/F*

You've gotta be positive. Your selling yourself. Its you against the world here man! **John** *(I)/F*

The most challenging thing is to make sure you are the best candidate in comparison to the other applicants. It is important to be positive and enthusiastic; however, at the same time always remain truthful. **Hannah** *I/F*

3 Read the comments again. Decide if they are informal (*I*) or formal (*F*).

4 Look at John's comment again.

Correct:
- spelling and grammar mistakes.
- punctuation mistakes.

Rewrite:
- shortened phrases out in full, eg *gonna = going to; we're = we are*.

Rewrite John's comment more formally below.

______

______

5 Read the article and comments again and answer these questions.

1 Which two things should you look at before an interview?
______ ______
2 When should you get to the interview?
Approximately ______ early.
3 Should you always wear a suit?
a yes   b no
4 Will everyone have very different qualifications?
   a Yes. The candidates will probably have very different educational backgrounds.
   b No. Most of the candidates will probably have similar educational backgrounds.
   c Yes, but only some will be hardworking. Others might be good at communicating.
5 Which comment is not related to a point in the article?
   a Lenny's
   b Ruby's
   c John's
   d Hannah's
6 Which points in the article (*Do your research / Arrive on time*, etc) are the other comments related to?
   1 ______'s comment: ______
   2 ______'s comment: ______
   3 ______'s comment: ______

GO BEYOND

Research a job you might be interested in doing in the future. What advice can you find on the internet about the qualifications and experience you'll need and the application process?

GRAMMAR 1 *Make*, *let* and *allow*

»» Talk about obligation and permission

1 Complete the rules for using *make*, *let* and *allow* with the words and phrases in the box.

allow   infinitive without *to*   infinitive with *to*
let   obligation   permission

make
Use: For (1) .... that comes from another person.
Form: *make* + object + (2) .... *They made me work long days.*
let **and** ***allow***
Use: For giving or not giving (3) .... (4) .... is more formal than (5) ....
Form: (*not*) *let* + object + infinitive without *to* *They let us go home early.*
(*not*) *allow* + object + (6) .... *They allowed us to go home early.*
be allowed
Use: To say you have or don't have permission.
Form: (*not*) *be allowed* + infinitive with *to* *You're not allowed to take long breaks.*

2 › Choose the correct sentence, a, b or c (two sentences in each group have mistakes).

1 a The teacher let us to watch a film.
  b The teacher let us watching a film.
  c The teacher let us watch a film.

2 a Under-14s* are not allowed to work.
  b Under-14s are not allowed working.
  c Under-14s are not allowed work.

Glossary
***Under-14s** = people under the age of 14

3 a She made us turning off our phones.
  b She made us turn off our phones.
  c She made us to turn off our phones.

4 a Her brother let her use his new MP3 player.
  b Her brother let her to use his new MP3 player.
  c Her brother let her using his new MP3 player.

5 a The teacher made Sam to do his homework.
  b The teacher made Sam doing his homework.
  c The teacher made Sam do his homework.

6 a The teacher allowed us leaving early.
  b The teacher allowed us to leaving early.
  c The teacher allowed us to leave early.

7 a I wasn't allowed to go running.
  b I wasn't allowed go running.
  c I wasn't allowed going running.

3 › Complete each pair of sentences below with *allow* or *be allowed*. Use a negative form for sentences with an ✗ and a positive form for sentences with a ✓.

1 ✓
   a My boss allows me to start work when I want.
   b We are allowed to start work when we want.

2 ✓
   a They ______ us five minutes of break time every hour.
   b We ______ a five-minute break every hour.

3 ✓
   a You ______ to eat at your desk.
   b They ______ us to eat at our desks.

4 ✗
   a We ______ to make private calls at work. It's forbidden.
   b My boss ______ private calls at work. They're forbidden.

5 ✗
   a The shop ______ me to buy things at a discount.
   b We ______ to buy things at a discount.

6 ✓
   a We ______ to park in the office car park.
   b They ______ us to park in the office car park.

4 › Choose the correct options to complete the email.

Hi Rita,

How's your work experience going? Mine's going OK but they are quite strict. We aren't (1) ***allow*** / ***allowed*** to talk when we're at our desks. They (2) ***allow*** / ***let*** us listen to music though, which is cool. We are (3) ***allowed*** / ***made*** to check lots of numbers. I get really tired but we are (4) ***allowed*** / ***allow*** to take lots of breaks. They won't let us sit still for more than an hour.

What does your work (5) ***make*** / ***allow*** you do? Do they give you a lot of work? What about the rules – are you (6) ***allowed*** / ***let*** lots of freedom?

Best wishes,

Jamie

5 ›› Rearrange the words to make sentences.

1 not / to / smoke / allowed / you're / on / plane / the / .
______
2 you / keep / this cream / I / let / can't / your / skin / for too long / on / .
______
3 out / you / not / get / are / allowed / of / bed / to / .
______
4 you / install / can't / product / I / let / that / .
______
5 in / allowed / eat / the computer room / you / are / to / not / .
______
6 it / again / director / made / them / the / do / .
______
7 save / the / me / money / accountant / made / .
______
8 work / parents / in / agriculture / made / me / my / .
______

6 ››› Use the prompts to write complete sentences. Use the pronoun *me* when necessary.

1 (my boss / allow / work from home)
   My boss allows me to work from home.
2 (they / not allow / any visitors)
______
3 (they / make / do the same thing all day)
______
4 (he / let / cook the starters)
______
5 (they / make / wash all the dishes)
______
6 (we / allow / to eat for free)
______

LISTENING

Infer meaning when you listen

1 Complete the tips with the phrases in the box.

Friends are likely to use humour	Identify the relationship between	Listen to how people talk	People are more careful with their words

REMEMBER HOW TO ...

infer meaning when you listen

If you infer meaning, you understand what people don't say directly.

- (1) .... Their voice often tells you what they really think. ☐
- (2) .... speakers. ☐
- (3) .... when they don't know or don't trust someone. ☐
- (4) .... and sometimes mean the opposite of what they say. ☐

2 Label the photos with the genre of film in the box.

horror	musical	thriller	western

1 ....

2 ....

3 ....

4 ....

3 15 Listen and write a genre of film from Exercise 2 next to each speaker.

Speaker 1 ....
Speaker 2 ....
Speaker 3 ....
Speaker 4 ....

4 16 Listen to each speaker talking about their job. Are they positive or negative about their job?

Speaker 1 *positive/negative*
Speaker 2 *positive/negative*
Speaker 3 *positive/negative*
Speaker 4 *positive/negative*

5 17 Listen to the speakers again. Does each speaker know and trust the person they are speaking to?

Speaker 1 *Yes/No*
Speaker 2 *Yes/No*
Speaker 3 *Yes/No*
Speaker 4 *Yes/No*

6 Which tips in the *Remember how to* box helped you in Exercises 4 and 5? Tick (✓) them.

VOCABULARY 2

4

Film jobs

1 Match each job (1–9) to its definition (a–i).

1 caterer ____ a a person who replaces someone else in a dangerous situation
2 costume designer ____ b a person with nothing or very little to say in a film, often in the background
3 dialogue coach ____ c a person providing the food
4 director ____ d a person in charge of the clothes
5 editor ____ e a person in charge of making a film, especially telling actors what to do
6 extra ____ f a person who helps actors with their words
7 make-up artist ____ g a person whose job it is to choose and arrange parts of a film
8 producer ____ h a person who organises the work and finds the money for a film
9 stunt double ____ i a person who looks after the appearance of the actors

2 Who would say this? Choose the correct person (a, b or c).

1 *We need to shoot this from a different angle.* a director b producer c editor

2 *I need to cut this down from two hours 30 minutes to under two hours.* a director b producer c editor

3 *These don't look like 1980s' clothes to me. They look more like something from the 70s.* a make-up artist b extra c costume designer

4 *We need to spend less on food. Can we find someone cheaper to provide the food?* a caterer b extra c producer

5 *Your accent isn't quite right. You sound Portuguese not Spanish.* a dialogue coach b make-up artist c stunt double

WORDS & BEYOND

3 Match the jobs (1–4) to the connected words (a–f). Some jobs will have more than one match.

1 accountant ____ a spreadsheet
2 beauty therapist ____ b manicure
3 veterinary nurse ____ c injection
4 flight attendant ____ d paperwork
e journey
f pedicure

4 Complete the conversation with the words in the box.

crowd scene film credits locations mates outfits set shoot zombie

Ed: Guess what. I've got a role in a film!
Nikki: Really? How did you get that?
Ed: One of my brother's (1) ____ is a director and they need some extras for their latest shoot.
Nikki: Cool! What are you going to (2) ____ ?
Ed: It's a (3) ____ movie. The (4) ____ are really terrifying!
Nikki: So what do you have to do?
Ed: It's a (5) ____ , so you might not even see me.
Nikki: Will you be in the (6) ____ at the end?
Ed: I think so.
Nikki: Where's it being filmed?
Ed: They're using lots of different (7) ____ , like London, New York, Sydney … .
Nikki: You're going to all of them?
Ed: No! I'm on a (8) ____ in London.

5 Complete the email with the words and phrases in the box.

blank crossroads harmful in a hurry salary scheme

Hi Michael,
How are you? Sorry I didn't have time to chat last time we met. I was (1) ____ to get home. I'm writing to ask you for some help. I'm at a (2) ____ and I can't decide which direction to take. How did you decide what you wanted? My mind is (3) ____ – I have no idea what to do. How's your apprenticeship (4) ____ going? Are they paying you a good (5) ____ ? Do you have to use any (6) ____ chemicals?
See you soon,
Tom

GRAMMAR 2 Defining and non-defining relative clauses

>>> Add extra information to a sentence

1 Complete the grammar table with the words and phrases in the box.

extra full stop people (x2) places possessions *that* the relative pronoun things

Defining relative clauses
Example: *A producer is someone who finds the money for a film.*
Use: To identify and describe (1) .... , things and places
Form: ■ Use *who/that* for (2) .... ■ Use *which/that* for (3) .... ■ Use *where* for (4) .... ■ Use *whose* for (5) ....
You can leave out the relative pronoun (*who*, etc) if the noun that would come before it is the object of the next verb. *Programmes (which) you watch online are becoming more popular.*
Non-defining relative clauses
Example: *The Harry Potter films, which are based on the books by JK Rowling, took many years to make.*
Use: To give (6) .... information.
Form: ■ They don't start with (7) .... ■ They have a comma at the start and a comma or (8) .... at the end. ■ You can't leave out (9) ....

2 › Correct the pronouns in these sentences.

1 She is the girl ~~which~~ plays the guitar in the band. *who/that*
2 He is the boy whose quit college last week. ....
3 This is the company who has five jobs advertised. ....
4 The other day I met a man who sister works in media. ....
5 He is a young film director which mother was a very famous actress. ....
6 I've got a job in a shop whose sells great cakes! ....

3 ›› Complete the conversation with *who*, *which* or *where*.

Gary: Shall we have something to drink?
Helen: Yes, but let's find a place (1) .... we can sit down. I don't want to go to a café (2) .... only has standing room.
Gary: I know a good place. Do you remember the boy (3) .... sat near the teacher in our maths class?
Helen: The one (4) .... wore glasses.
Gary: Yes, I saw him in a café the other day. It's one (5) .... you can get a free refill of your coffee.
Helen: Sounds good. Where is it?
Gary: It's one of those ones (6) .... you can enter from South Street or King Street.

4 ›› Complete the second sentence so that it has a similar meaning to the first.

1 I had to attend a meeting. It went on for three hours.
The meeting *I had to attend went on* for three hours.
2 See that house over there. My parents live in it.
That's .... live in.
3 The police officer was chasing a man. He lost sight of him.
The policeman .... he was chasing.
4 I chose the numbers. They didn't win a prize.
The numbers .... didn't win a prize.
5 It's a great job. Everyone wants it.
It's .... wants.
6 Sally baked some cakes. They were delicious.
The cakes .... delicious.

5 ››› Combine the information in brackets with the first sentence. Use *who*, *whose* or *which*.

1 An accountant has gone to prison. (He stole millions of pounds from clients.)
The *accountant who stole millions of pounds from clients has gone to prison.*
2 The carpenter was very cheap. (He fitted new doors in our house.)
The ....
3 My friend's bike was stolen. (He walked to work.)
My ....
4 The clothes store has closed down. (I loved it.)
The ....
5 A runner has been banned from the Olympics. (He cheated.)
The ....
6 The estate agent has lost his job. (He sold my house.)
The ....
7 The florist is really good. (She did the flowers at my wedding.)
The ....
8 The lawyer is expensive. (He dealt with my legal problem.)
The ....

Check and correct understanding

1 a Label the photos with the words in the box.

caterer electrician veterinary nurse

1

2

3
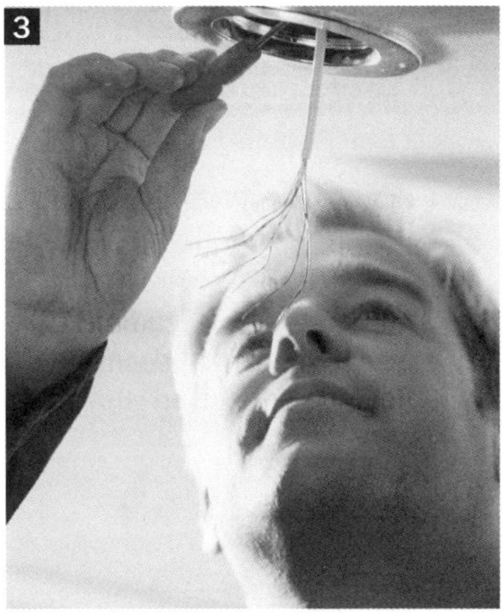

....

b What do you think would be difficult about learning to do each of these jobs? Write notes in your notebook.

2 ▶18 Listen to the first part of the conversation. Which job from Exercise 1 are they learning to do?

....

3 a Complete the *Phrasebook* with the words in the box.

correct meant other saying (x2) with

b ▶19 Now listen and check.

4 ▶20 Listen and repeat the phrases, paying attention to intonation.

5 Imagine a difficult situation in one of the jobs in Exercise 1, or another job you know well. Write a conversation that includes at least six phrases from the *Phrasebook*.

A: ....
B: ....
A: ....
B: ....
A: ....
B: ....

6 Record yourself saying one of the speaker's sentences in your conversation. Play the sentences back and say the responses from your conversation.

PHRASEBOOK

Checking you have understood

In (1) .... words, ...
You're (2) .... that ...
Do you mean ... ?
So, ...
Are you saying that ...
Can I check something?

Checking you have been understood

Do you understand what I'm (3) .... ?
Stop me if you don't understand.
Are you (4) .... me?
Have you got the idea?
Do you follow?

Confirming or correcting understanding

That's not what I (5) ....
What I'm saying is ...
That's (6) ....
I'm not sure you've understood.
You've got it.

WRITING

Write a formal letter

1 a **Can you remember the rules for writing a formal letter? Close your *Workbook* and write the ones you can remember in your notebook.**

b **Choose the correct option to complete the tips.**

REMEMBER HOW TO ...

write a formal letter

- Follow the writing rules in Exercise 3.
- Write *full forms* / *contractions* .
- Use formal words and phrases whenever possible.

2 **Read the letter and answer the questions below.**

11 Olle Close
Ipswich
IP33 2NW
29th May

Relax Health and Beauty
19 Queens Drive
Ipswich
IP28 2CP

Dear Sir or Madam,
I am writing regarding the apprenticeship in Relax Health and Beauty which I saw advertised at the local college.

I am currently studying Health and Beauty full time, but I will shortly finish the course. I am hoping to gain more practical experience to go with the knowledge and skills I have already acquired. I know that Relax Health and Beauty is the premier beautician's in the region and I would very much like to further my skills under your supervision.

Please find enclosed my CV with further details of my qualifications and experience. I am available for interview at any time. I hope you will consider me for the apprenticeship. I look forward to hearing from you.

Yours faithfully,
Callum Gerard

1 Where did Callum find out about the apprenticeship?

....

2 When does Callum's course end?

....

3 What has he put in the envelope with the letter?

....

3 **Choose the correct option to complete the rules for writing formal letters.**

1 Write your address at the *top right* / *top left* .
2 Write the date after *your address* / *the company address* .
3 Write the name and address of the person you're writing to on the *right* / *left* at the top of the page.
4 Start your letter with *Hi Mr/Mrs/Ms ...* / *Dear Mr/Mrs/Ms ...* . If you don't know the person's name, just write *Dear Sir or Madam* / *Hi there* .
5 End your letter with the phrase *Write back soon* / *I look forward to hearing from you* .
6 Above your signature write *Cheers* / *Yours faithfully* if you don't know the person's name and *Yours sincerely* / *Love* if you do.

4 **Look at the job advert and answer the questions below.**

EXTRAS NEEDED. Must be willing to travel, and work long and irregular hours. Send your CV and covering letter to: Tom Smith, 20 Broad Street, London, SW1 8TY.

1 Which two of these characteristics are important for the job?
   a hardworking
   b flexible
   c creative
2 How would you start your letter?
   a Hi Tom
   b Dear Mr Smith
   c Dear Sir or Madam

WRITING PLAN

5 **You're going to write a letter in response to the job advert in Exercise 4. Remember to use the rules for writing a formal letter. Use the *Writing plan* to help you prepare.**

WRITING PLAN

Make notes for your letter.

Paragraph 1: Say why you're writing and where you saw the advert. ☐

Paragraph 2: Describe the skills and experience you have which would be good for this job, and give some examples. ☐

Paragraph 3: Say when you can start, how many hours you can work and when. Tell them if you can travel for work. ☐

Paragraph 4: End your letter in a formal way. ☐

WRITE AND CHECK

6 **Write your letter. Then tick (✓) the stages in the *Writing plan*.**

Think ahead and make plans

1 **Read the tips on thinking ahead and making plans. Put them in a logical order from 1–7.**

a Plan how to reach your dreams. ____
b Think about your strengths, your dreams and what you want from life. ____
c Write these – your strengths and dreams – down. ____
d Find somewhere quiet where you can concentrate. *1*
e Put your plan somewhere you can see it to remind yourself of your goals. ____
f Ignore negative thoughts and people – keep going with your plan and start to speak about your future in the present. ____
g Start to put your plan into action – and go to the place you put your notes to read them again at least once every day. ____

2 **Read this situation. Do you think Liz will achieve her dreams or not? Why?**

MY BLOG

'Ever since I was very young I wanted to become a fashion designer. I didn't just sit there and draw pictures, or spend all my time shopping, I spent time researching the career. I found out very quickly that it's really competitive and very few people are successful, but I also found out exactly what you need to do. I know the best courses to take at school and the best university to go to. I've also taken lots of extra creative courses in design, photography and technology. Some of my teachers haven't been very positive though. They say I'm not very creative and that I should look for another profession. I've started to look at graphic design as I'm good with computers.'

3 **What advice would you give Liz?**

GET ORGANISED

1 Complete the sentences with the words/phrases in the box, using the singular or plural form as necessary.

avalanche drought earthquake flood hurricane
landslide tornado tsunami volcanic eruption wildfire

1 A(n) ______ is often caused by a(n) ______ underneath the sea. The waves head towards land and ______ the surrounding area.
2 A(n) ______ is caused by a powerful thunderstorm that produces extremely strong spinning winds. A(n) ______ is a huge storm that brings heavy winds and rain to a large area.
3 ______s are made up of lots of stones, mud and rocks moving down a hill or mountain, whereas ______s usually consist of snow and ice.
4 When there is a(n) ______ and an area becomes very dry, a(n) ______ can occur in very hot temperatures, especially in forests.
5 Even though ______s are dangerous, many people live near these dangerous mountains because the land is good for crops.

2 Choose the action that DOESN'T match the sound. Choose one option only, a, b or c.

1 crash
a two cars hitting each other
b a yoghurt landing on the floor
c a ball going through a window

2 burst
a a bike tyre going over glass
b a balloon touching a sharp stone
c a vase landing on the floor

3 groan
a a sound when you're excited
b a sound when you're unhappy
c a sound when you're in pain

4 roar
a a pet cat
b a lion
c a motorbike

5 slam
a a phone being put down angrily
b a bomb going off
c a door being closed loudly

6 sigh
a a sound when you're tired
b a sound when you're upset
c a sound when you're interested in something

3 Choose the word or phrase that does not collocate with the verb.

1	*achieve*	fame	the top	an ambition	a dream
2	*encounter*	your potential	difficulties	a problem	an issue
3	*face*	your fears	an ambition	difficulties	a challenge
4	*fulfil*	an invitation	your potential	a dream	an ambition
5	*overcome*	problems	obstacles	your goal	difficulties
6	*risk*	your life	problems	everything	your money
7	*take*	a risk	fame	a chance	an action
8	*take up*	an offer	a challenge	an invitation	your life

4 Complete the sentences with a verb from Exercise 3 and a word/phrase from the box.

a challenge a risk everything fame your fears your potential

1 Psychologists often say that you should ______ . It can help make them less of a problem.
2 Many people want to ______ , but find life difficult when they get their wish and have no privacy.
3 If you don't practise, you won't be able to ______ . Top sports people practise for hours every day.
4 You're always so careful in life. Why don't you ______ for a change?
5 Don't ______ you have on this. You might lose it all.
6 Every year I like to ______ . Last year I ran a marathon; next year I'm swimming 50 kilometres.

ALL ABOUT ME

1 What would you rather achieve – fame or a different ambition? Why?

______

2 Do you have any fears? Have you ever tried to overcome them?

______

3 Would you risk everything to fulfil your most important dream?

______

1 Complete each sentence with a relative pronoun and the correct form of *make, let* or *be allowed*.

1 Mountain biking is a sport *which/that lets* you explore away from the roads.
2 The flight attendant is the person ______ you sit down when there is turbulence on the flight.
3 A director is a person ______ actors perform in a certain way.
4 A set is a place ______ actors ______ to change who they are for a while.
5 A tsunami is an event ______ people leave their homes quickly.
6 Facebook is a website ______ you tag people in photos.
7 Firefighters are the people ______ local residents leave their homes in a wildfire situation.
8 In the book *1984*, Big Brother is a person ______ people follow the rules.

2 Join the two sentences together. Use *when* and the past perfect.

1 The students did a questionnaire. Then they wrote a report.
When the students had done a questionnaire, they wrote a report.
2 Monty saved enough money. Then he got a new games console.
______
3 I read the book. I took it back to the library.
______
4 Mark went mountain biking for the afternoon. Then his parents went to the shops.
______
5 I looked both ways. Then I crossed the road.
______
6 Gemma didn't return my call. So I texted her.
______

3 Look at these sentences and tick (✓) the correct answer, a or b.

1 Harry and Amelia were talking together when Lisa yelled at them.
Which took longer? a ☐ what Harry and Amelia said
b ☐ what Lisa said

2 Taka had finished his essay, but Tommy was still working on his presentation.
Which was finished first? a ☐ writing the essay
b ☐ preparing the presentation

3 Lily got home and switched on the TV.
What did she do first? a ☐ get home
b ☐ switch on the TV

4 When Sarah got to school, she finished her homework.
When did she finish her homework? a ☐ before getting to school
b ☐ after getting to school

5 'I was watching TV when the phone rang.'
Which started first? a ☐ watching TV
b ☐ the phone ringing

6 We had already got everyone out when the firefighters arrived.
When did they get everyone out? a ☐ before the firefighters arrived
b ☐ after the firefighters arrived

UNIT 5

STREET ART

VOCABULARY 1 Talk about different types of art

1 Complete the networks with the words in the box.

bridge brush canvas instrument novel orchestra
poem skyscraper stage stone theatre wood

1 **actor**

2 **musician**

3 **architect**

4 **writer**

5 **sculptor**

6 **painter**

2 Match the types of art (1–10) to the descriptions (a–j).

1 portrait	a a message or image sprayed onto a wall
2 landscape	b a painting of natural objects such as a bowl of fruit or flowers
3 performance art	c a functional object put in a gallery or museum
4 still life	d a quick drawing
5 mural	e different materials or photos put together
6 sketch	f a drawing done on the ground
7 pavement art	g a painting painted directly onto a wall
8 collage	h a picture of a person
9 graffiti	i art created using the artist's body
10 installation art	j a picture of the countryside

3 Complete the sentences with seven of the words from Exercise 2.

1 *I had to sit still for ages while my .... was painted.*

2 *It's called .... art but, to me, it's just a real telephone on an empty desk.*

3 *What I like about that .... is that the apples look real enough to eat.*

4 *We had five minutes to use our pencil to make a .... of what we saw.*

5 .... *looks wonderful, but if people walk over it or it rains, it's destroyed.*

6 *Ah! Clouds and sea! What a fine .... painting that is.*

7 *Can an artist sleeping in a glass box in a gallery really be called .... art?*

4 Choose the correct option to complete the sentences.

1 The original sculpture is in the British Museum. This is a(n) ***ink*** / ***plaster*** copy.
2 It's amazing how lifelike she makes it just with ink and ***collage*** / ***paper***.
3 It's all done with the same sort of ***chalk*** / ***canvas*** our teachers use to write on the board.
4 Most graffiti is done with ***oil*** / ***spray*** paint.

READING

Transfer information to a different text

1 Complete the tips with the words in the box.

REMEMBER HOW TO …

transfer information to a different text

formal	information	purpose
quote	sentences	sources

- Identify the (1) __________ of the new text, who the readers are and which (2) __________ is important.
- Decide if the text should be notes or full (3) __________ .
- Decide if the style is (4) __________ or informal.
- Use your own words. Give (5) __________ if you (6) __________ or copy information.

2 Read the text and choose where it's from.

a a news report
b a guidebook
c an advertisement
d a novel

FLORENCE: TOP TEN HIGHLIGHTS?

Michelangelo's David

Walking around Florence, you will eventually end up in the main square, the Piazza della Signoria, and there you will find a copy of one of the most famous statues in the world – Michelangelo's *David* (which was created from a huge old piece of marble that the artist worked on for over two years before finally finishing it in 1504). *(1)* It had been commissioned by the Florentine authorities to be put as one of a series of statues on the roof of the cathedral, but instead because it was too big and heavy to be lifted there, it was placed in the square with David's eyes looking towards Rome. The message was simple: Florence, like David, was surrounded by giant powerful cities, but would be strong and win, if it came under attack.

3 Decide which of the following is the missing sentence that goes at (1) in the Exercise 2 text.

a He had been ill as a child, which shows you how hard he tried.
b I couldn't have done that – could you?
c The original, which stands over five metres tall, is now in the nearby Accademia Gallery.

4 Tick (✓) which piece of information, a or b, is suitable for adding to the text *Florence: Top Ten Highlights*.

1 a Wow! The size of that statue is unbelievable! ☐
  b In fact, just to get it to the square from the artist's studio was a huge task. ☐
2 a The guide said it was some sort of a political statement, but I don't understand how. ☐
  b Perhaps this was a warning or political message to potential enemies. ☐
3 a However, *David* is not the only statue in the square. ☐
  b It's raining here at the moment. ☐
4 a Public art – art that can be seen in public outside spaces – has several purposes. ☐
  b It's been here for over 500 years, she said. ☐
5 a Such art may help people to remember a great person or event, or celebrate a place. ☐
  b But the street performers are cheering us up. ☐

5 The five sentences you didn't choose in Exercise 4 are comments on a tourist's social networking site. Write the sentences below in a logical order.

1	*It's raining here at the moment.*	13:05
2	__________	13:06
3	__________	13:10
4	__________	13:11
5	__________	13:12

6 Which sentence(s) in Exercise 5 do(es) not transfer information from the text in Exercise 2? __________

7 Put the sentences (a–c) in the right place in the texts (1–3).

Text 1 ____

Ladies and gentlemen, welcome to the Ruskin lecture. The great man once said that the most beautiful things in life are the most useless. (1) In fact, it's the most useful thing we have to help us make sense of our odd world.

Text 2 ____

9:30

When I get in, let's meet under the bean – you know – that huge silver sculpture in the middle of the square. (2) See you.

REPLY

Text 3 ____

David – Michelangelo – Florence – 1504 – (3) – copy in square

a I'll text you when the train arrives, OK?
b I am here today to argue that art is not about beauty.
c original in Accademia

GO BEYOND

Take a photo of a piece of street art near where you live or find one in your nearest city on the internet. Describe it and say what you think about it.

GRAMMAR 1 *-ing* forms

Use gerunds and participle clauses

1 Complete the grammar table with the words in the box.

clauses   main   noun   object   subject (x2)   time   verb

Gerunds
Use: As a (1) ....
Form: Gerunds can be either the (2) .... or the (3) .... of a sentence.
Present participles
Use: As a (4) .... to connect two (5) .... in a sentence.
Form: Use a present participle if: ■ two things happen at the same (6) .... ■ the (7) .... clause and participle have the same (8) ....

2 Decide if the *-ing* form in these sentences is a noun (*N*) or a verb (*V*).

1 Francisco de Pájaro likes making art from rubbish. ....
2 Finding some rubbish on the street, he thinks about what he could make from it. ....
3 He puts the bits of rubbish together using tape and paints it. ....
4 Some of his works take human forms, looking like famous people. ....
5 While he works, people often gather around wondering who he is. ....
6 Having his art in the street means more people see it than if it was in a gallery. ....

3 › Choose the correct options to complete the sentences.

1 Always wash your brushes after ***paint*** / ***painting*** so they ***are*** / ***being*** ready for the next time.
2 When ***thinking*** / ***think*** about what to draw, I ***going*** / ***go*** for a walk in the park.
3 Before ***take*** / ***taking*** a photograph, I ***look*** / ***looking*** at the object from different angles.
4 After ***finish*** / ***finishing*** a painting, I ***putting*** / ***put*** my signature on the canvas.
5 I usually ***listen*** / ***listening*** to music while ***painting*** / ***paint***.
6 Picasso said he ***being*** / ***was*** only able to paint like a child after ***study*** / ***studying*** art for years.

4 › Rearrange the words to make statements from some famous artists. Clue: Start each sentence with the word in bold.

1 *only / alive / I / when / **The** / painting / time / feel / is / .* (Vincent van Gogh)

The only time I feel alive is when painting.

2 *home / is / **Art** / only way / leaving / run away / to / without / the / .* (Twyla Tharp)

3 *paint / **I** dream of / my dream / then / and / painting / I / .* (Vincent van Gogh)

4 *but very difficult / don't know how, / **Painting** / when you do / is / when / you / easy / .* (Edgar Degas)

5 *making / think / **Don't** / about / art, just / it done / get / .* (Andy Warhol)

6 *poetry / is seen / that / **Painting** / is / than / rather / felt / .* (Leonardo da Vinci)

7 *thing / **Making** your unknown known / is / most important / the / .* (Georgia O'Keeffe)

5 ›› Complete the sentences with a word or phrase from the box and the correct form of the verbs in brackets.

a helpful older sister	a work of art	homework
in public	the news	~~this movie~~	to concerts

1 (Make) *Making this movie* was a really fun experience.
2 (Have) ______ means I'm a very lucky person.
3 (Do) ______ on your own isn't much fun.
4 (Create) ______ takes time and patience.
5 (Get) ______ isn't easy as I live in a mountain village.
6 (Speak) ______ used to frighten me when I was younger.
7 (Watch) ______ every day keeps me up to date with what's happening.

6 ››› Complete the conversation using the correct form of the verbs in brackets. Use the present simple, past simple or the *-ing* form.

Katrin: What do you think of my sculpture? I (1) ______ (make) it (2) ______ (use) stuff I (3) ______ (found) in the street. I (4) ______ (love) (5) ______ (look) around for things that have been thrown away, (6) ______ (make) them 'live' again.

Osil: OK, so what's it supposed to be?

Katrin: An old woman (7) ______ (sit) in a doorway (8) ______ (hold) a doll.

LISTENING

Recognise general statements and exceptions

1 Complete the phrases with the words in the box. (Don't worry about the lines on the right yet.)

apart except exception general large most rule whole

1 With the ____________ of a few people, *E*
2 In ____________ , ____
3 ____________ people think that ... ____
4 As a ____________ , ____
5 ____________ from ... ____
6 By and ____________ , ____
7 ____________ for ... ____
8 On the ____________ , ____

REMEMBER HOW TO ...

recognise general statements and exceptions

General statements say something is true in most situations, but there may be exceptions.

2 Look back at the phrases in Exercise 1. Decide if they are for general statements (*G*) or for exceptions (*E*). The first one has been done for you.

3 Match the types of art (a–d) to the photos (1–4).

1 

2 

3 

4 

a graffiti
b installation art
c trash art
d performance art

4 21 Listen and write the type of art from Exercise 3 that each speaker is talking about.

Speaker 1 ____________
Speaker 2 ____________
Speaker 3 ____________
Speaker 4 ____________

5 21 Listen again. Match these general statements to the speakers. Write *Speaker 1*, etc.

1 They like what I do. ____________
2 They sat on the usual thing there. ____________
3 It's wrong to commit a crime. ____________
4 I usually play Bach. ____________

6 21 Listen again. Which speaker doesn't speak about an exception?

Speaker ____

7 22 Listen to four speakers talking about their visit to an art gallery. What does each speaker say is an exception? Match the speakers (1–4) to the statements (a–d).

Speaker 1 ____
Speaker 2 ____
Speaker 3 ____
Speaker 4 ____

a There was nowhere to buy things.
b A particular artist's good work.
c Art which has a clear meaning.
d A particular painter's bad work.

VOCABULARY 2

5

Words to describe art

1 Match 1–12 to a–l to make adjectives.

1	con	a	pressive
2	aver	b	ful
3	im	c	ing
4	power	d	que
5	sub	e	orate
6	dram	f	ning
7	mov	g	tle
8	elab	h	troversial
9	uni	i	age
10	stun	j	atic
11	quir	k	ll
12	du	l	ky

2 Choose the best options to complete the conversation.

Bob: I thought the costumes were absolutely (1) ***stunning*** / ***dull*** . The designer should get an award – a prize or something.

Mark: Yes, but it was the voices – how (2) ***elaborate*** / ***powerful*** and strong they were – that I really loved.

Bob: Certainly, considering they didn't use microphones. It's a bit (3) ***average*** / ***controversial*** that, isn't it? Should you use microphones in a live opera performance in the theatre or not?

Mark: Well, they didn't, and the sound was (4) ***subtle*** / ***impressive*** . I heard every note.

Bob: What I find amazing is that – not just in opera, but generally (it's true for pop and rock as well) – you can tell who's singing. Everyone has a(n) (5) ***unique*** / ***average*** voice.

Mark: Quite true. There are (6) ***dull*** / ***subtle*** ways you use your voice that make it distinctively* yours.

Glossary
***distinctively** = clearly

3 Complete the sentences with the words in the box.

average dramatic dull
elaborate moving quirky

1 It was so boring; I fell asleep after twenty minutes. How ________ that was!
2 It made me cry. It was so ________ when she sang the last song and died.
3 The ________ costumes, with all that detail, must have taken ages to make.
4 Wasn't it ________ when he arrived suddenly from out of the sky?
5 I didn't think much of it really. I'd give it two stars – just a(n) ________ film.
6 Burt Timon's films are always ________ – there's something a bit strange and different about them.

WORDS & BEYOND

4 Find nine words in the word search and use them to complete the sentences below.

C	H	A	R	C	O	A	L	P	X
M	S	V	U	E	B	J	X	S	G
D	U	W	L	K	L	A	H	C	L
R	W	G	E	G	R	A	L	Q	T
P	N	E	Z	B	O	W	M	U	H
A	E	P	M	C	W	H	E	U	W
X	C	F	S	L	K	O	Q	D	D
S	N	E	I	Y	S	L	L	F	G
Q	R	U	J	L	R	E	A	V	Z
F	E	N	O	Z	Z	X	A	Z	N

1 On the w _ _ _ _ , I agree with you.
2 I do my pavement art with many colours of c _ _ _ _ .
3 One type of wall art is a f _ _ _ _ _ .
4 I did a still l _ _ _ once and the apples looked more like oranges.
5 From this a _ _ _ _ it looks like a skull.
6 If you find things unusual, you may be out of your comfort z _ _ _ .
7 By and l _ _ _ _ , I think going to art school was worth it.
8 Put your handprint in m _ _ and then let it dry.
9 I think c _ _ _ _ _ _ _ is made from burnt wood, isn't it?

5 Complete the email with the words in the box.

angle concerned generally
images imagination unfamiliar

Hi Jane,

You said your teacher had told you all to use your (1) ________ , but you can't think of anything new for your art project. Don't worry. Why don't you look at some art from other cultures? As far as I'm (2) ________ , that's where we have to look to make something new for ourselves. Looking at things that are (3) ________ to us can help us see things from a different (4) ________ . It's (5) ________ accepted that Picasso got ideas from African masks, so why don't you search the internet for (6) ________ of art from places far away? You might find something to get you going.

Good luck,

Lucy

GRAMMAR 2 Question tags

>>> Ask questions and confirm ideas using question tags

1 Complete the grammar table with the words in the box.

auxiliary confirm do end negative positive questions

Question tags
Use: ■ To ask questions and (1) .... ideas. ■ At the (2) .... of sentences to make (3) ....
Form: ■ Use a positive question tag with a (4) .... sentence. *You haven't seen my glasses anywhere, have you?*
■ Use a negative question tag with a (5) .... sentence. *He can't draw a straight line, can he?*
■ Make the question tag using the (6) .... verb from the first part of the sentence + subject. *We won't miss the start, will we?*
■ If there is no auxiliary verb, use the correct form of the verb (7) .... *They know where to go, don't they?*

Note: To make a suggestion, you can use *Let's … , shall we?*
Let's go for a walk, shall we?

2 > Choose the correct sentence, a, b or c.

1 a You left early, left you?
 b You left early, didn't you?
 c You left early, do you?
2 a That was a silly thing to do, wasn't it?
 b That was a silly thing to do, didn't it?
 c That was a silly thing to do, was it?
3 a They can't be serious, can they?
 b They can't be serious, do they?
 c They can't be serious, can't they?
4 a You didn't tell anyone, didn't you?
 b You didn't tell anyone, did you?
 c You didn't tell anyone, have you?
5 a It'll be alright, be it?
 b It'll be alright, won't it?
 c It'll be alright, will it?
6 a Let's talk about this like adults, shall we?
 b Let's talk about this like adults, let us?
 c Let's talk about this like adults, won't we?

3 >> Correct the question tags in the sentences.

1 You've been painting, ~~aren't you?~~ *haven't you?*
2 That can't be a real Picasso, does it? ....
3 You don't think she really looks like that, don't you? ....
4 They went to the theatre last night, haven't they? ....
5 We're going next Friday, won't we? ....
6 You will remember to book, aren't you? ....
7 Let's have a break, will we? ....

4 >> Complete the conversation with the correct question tags.

Artur: You don't happen to know what's on at the National Theatre, (1) .... ?
Maya: No idea, but we could check on their website, (2) .... ?
Artur: Of course. There's usually something worth seeing, (3) .... ?
Maya: Right. I'll have a look. If I find something, I'll call you tonight, (4) .... ?
Artur: Fine. Oh, I nearly forgot. You couldn't lend me that history of theatre book, (5) .... ?
Maya: Certainly. How's the essay going? You wanted it to help with that, (6) .... ?
Artur: Yes, I'm a bit stuck, so it will be a big help to have it.

5 a >>> Match the statements (1–6) to the questions with a similar meaning (a–f). (Ignore the missing words for now.)

1 I can't believe someone paid a million dollars for that! *c*
2 I wonder what it's supposed to be – what's your view? ....
3 Perhaps it's trying to say something about the modern world. ....
4 I expect this isn't the first time you've seen her work. ....
5 If I remember rightly, there was an exhibition a few years ago. ....
6 This isn't anything new in my opinion. ....

a It's just the same old stuff, ... ?
b You've probably seen her work before, ... ?
c It's not worth so much, ... ?
d It might be attempting to tell us about life today, ... ?
e There was a show a few years ago, ... ?
f You can't tell me what you think that's supposed to be, ... ?

b Now write the correct question tags for questions a–f.

SPEAKING

Agree or disagree with an opinion

1 ▶23 Listen to four conversations. What are the people talking about? Match the conversations to the photos.

Conversation 1: ____ Conversation 2: ____ Conversation 3: ____ Conversation 4: ____

2 a Complete the *Phrasebook* with the words in the box.

actually afraid awful concerned do (x2) honest so totally

b ▶23 Listen again and check your answers.

3 ▶23 Listen again and write the correct conversation number(s) next to each question.

1 In which conversation(s) do the people agree about everything? ____
2 In which conversation(s) do the people disagree about everything? ____
3 In which conversation(s) do the people agree and disagree? ____

4 a Read the conversations and guess which phrases go in the gaps.

Conversation 1
John: Great last night, wasn't it? (1) ____ the guitarist in the last group was fantastic. Really talented.
Kat: (2) ____ . The singer wasn't all that good though. I think he wasn't confident enough and didn't really perform – just stood there with his eyes closed most of the time.
John: (3) ____ , that's just his style.

Conversation 2
Jane: What about these? Shall I go for the light blue ones or the black pair?
Petra: (4) ____ , black's best. You don't have to wash them so often, do you? And I (5) ____ they make you look slimmer.
Jane: (6) ____ . I'll just go and try them on.

Conversation 3
Pete: Isn't it awful so far? I didn't expect it to be so slow from the trailer I saw.
Doug: (7) ____ . I suppose the effects are good, but there's not much action so far, is there?
Pete: (8) ____ . Let's hope it's better after the break. Shall we get some popcorn?
Doug: Good idea – and a drink.

Conversation 4
Eva: I don't believe that you need an expensive camera. You can get really good shots with your smartphone.
Georgi: (9) ____ you there. Look at these wildlife pictures. You couldn't get that sort of quality without good equipment.
Eva: (10) ____ , I think it's more about being in the right place at the right time, not carrying around heavy expensive cameras with all these different lenses they have.

b ▶23 Listen again and check your answers.

PHRASEBOOK

Giving an opinion
I think/(1) ____ (that) ...
As far as I'm (2) ____ ...
Isn't it great/(3) ____ ... ?

Agreeing
I (4) ____ agree.
So (5) ____ I.
Neither (6) ____ I.
I think (7) ____ too.

Disagreeing
To be (8) ____ , ...
I'm (9) ____ I don't agree.
Well, (10) ____ ...

5 ▶24 Listen and repeat the phrases, paying special attention to stress and intonation.

6 Write a conversation about one of the statements below. Try to use at least six of the phrases from the *Phrasebook* for giving opinions, agreeing and disagreeing.

- Art has to be beautiful to be good.
- Soon, there won't be books because you can already read everything on the internet.
- It's wrong to download music for free.

A: ____
B: ____
A: ____
B: ____
A: ____
B: ____

7 Read your conversation aloud, paying special attention to the key phrases. Record yourself if you can.

WRITING

Use linking words

1 Match the sentence halves to complete the tips.

REMEMBER HOW TO …

use linking words

1	To add ideas, use	a	*so, as a result.*
2	To contrast ideas, use	b	*and, also, too.*
3	To express a cause, use	c	*but, however, although, even though.*
4	To express a result, use	d	*because, because of.*

2 Match the words (a–d) to the uses (1–4) in Exercise 1.

a *as* ……
b *therefore* ……
c *not only … but also* ……
d *despite* ……

3 Complete the gaps (a–g) with the words in the box. (Ignore options 1–10 for now.)

bands communities costumes police spectators sunshine tradition

Notting Hill Carnival

The Notting Hill Carnival is Europe's largest street party (1) ***and*** / ***but*** this year it attracted a million (a) …………… , watching the dancing and (2) ***also*** / ***too*** joining in. (3) ***Despite*** / ***Although*** the London weather can't always be relied upon, this year the party was held in brilliant (b) …………… .

The festival was started in the 1960s by people originally from the Caribbean (4) ***so*** / ***as*** they wanted to keep the carnival (c) …………… from their islands alive. (5) ***However*** / ***Even though***, for decades, people from all the (d) …………… of the city have been taking part in the fun.

There are groups of dancers in stunning, brightly coloured (e) …………… all dancing through the streets behind open trucks carrying steel drum (f) …………… . Giant sound systems play (6) ***and*** / ***not only*** the traditional calypso and soca music, (7) ***but also*** / ***therefore*** reggae, dub and much more to get the crowds going.

(8) ***Despite*** / ***Even though*** the general good mood, there are always a few problems reported by the (g) …………… , (9) ***because*** / ***but***, on the whole, it's a great experience, (10) ***so*** / ***because of*** I'll be back there next year!

4 Read the text in Exercise 3 again. Choose the correct options for 1–10.

WRITING PLAN

5 a You're going to write a story about a trip to another country. The story must begin or end with the following words: *What an adventure!* First, look at questions 1–6 below. Write them in the most appropriate paragraph of your *Writing plan*.

1 When did you go?
2 How do you feel about it now?
3 Was it a good or bad adventure? Why?
4 Where did you go?
5 Who did you meet there?
6 What happened?

WRITING PLAN

Make notes for your story.

Paragraph 1:
Question: *When did you go?* ☐
Question: ......
Notes: ......
Paragraph 2:
Question: ...... ☐
Question: ......
Notes: ......
Paragraph 3:
Question: ...... ☐
Notes: ......
Paragraph 4:
Question: ...... ☐
Notes: ......
Remember: Start or end your story with the phrase: *What an adventure!* ☐

b Now make notes to answer the questions.

WRITE AND CHECK

6 Write your story. Then tick (✓) the stages in the *Writing plan*.

Value the art and culture of different societies

1 Read the tips for keeping an open mind about other cultures. Tick (✓) them according to the key.

✓✓✓ = I often do this.
✓✓ = I've only done this once or twice.
✓ = I've never done this but would like to.

1 Try foods from different countries. ☐
2 Listen to music from a different culture. ☐
3 Visit a museum which has an exhibition of art from another country. ☐
4 Watch TV programmes from or about other countries. ☐
5 Write to someone in another country on a social networking site. ☐
6 Read a book translated into your language from another one. ☐

2 Add three more tips of your own.

1 ......
2 ......
3 ......

3 Read the comments and decide if what the people say shows an open mind (*O*) or a closed mind (*C*).

1 I don't see the point in ballroom dancing. It's certainly not for young people and anyway, we've got our own dance traditions here. ____
2 We had a school trip to Rome and were forced to go to all these boring old museums and landmarks. ____
3 I'm off to see the Native Australian art exhibition. I'm really interested in the natives' idea of dream time and I'm sure I'll learn more from the show. ____

4 Match the responses to the statements in Exercise 3.

____ a So aren't you at all interested in some of the greatest art and architecture ever produced?
____ b How can you say that before you've tried it? It could be lots of fun and good exercise.
____ c I've seen some images reproduced on T-shirts, but tell me about the ideas behind the art.

1 Add the prefixes *un-*, *im-*, *il-*, *in-* or *ir-* to form negative adjectives.

1 ____patient
2 ____relevant
3 ____well
4 ____capable
5 ____moral
6 ____legal
7 ____aware
8 ____logical

2 Match the negative adjectives from Exercise 1 to the meanings (a–h).

a against the law ____
b not connected to a subject being discussed ____
c not having the ability to do something ____
d not feeling healthy ____
e not knowing something is going on ____
f something which is thought by most people to be wrong ____
g not able to wait calmly for something to happen ____
h not reasonable; an unwise choice ____

3 Match 1–8 to a–h to make jobs.

1 software
2 make-up
3 park
4 beauty
5 estate
6 veterinary
7 flight
8 sound

a technician
b developer
c therapist
d ranger
e agent
f attendant
g artist
h nurse

4 Complete the paragraph with the words in the box.

access digital hands identity issue privacy reveal track

In this (1) ____ age, we enjoy (2) ____ to just about anything we want, which is great, but one big (3) ____ is that of (4) ____ . We don't know which individuals or organisations can (5) ____ our mobile and internet communications or who they (6) ____ our identity to. How easy is it for personal information to get into the wrong (7) ____ or even for our (8) ____ to be stolen?

5 Complete the paragraph with the words in the box.

achieve attempt avalanche encounter landslide risk stunning unlikely

I was prepared to (1) ____ everything to (2) ____ my ambition – to climb Mount Everest. It is something I had wanted to (3) ____ to do since I was a child. I (4) ____ed many problems to begin with when I tried to organise my trip, but eventually everything was in place and I was ready to go. Besides, organisational issues were not my big concern. I was more worried about the risk of (5) ____s and (6) ____s. And now here I was – finally on top of the world. The view was (7) ____ and I knew I was (8) ____ ever to forget this moment for so long as I lived.

ALL ABOUT ME

1 Which of the jobs from Exercise 3 would you most/least like to do? Why?

____

2 What's the longest time you've spent without using your mobile phone/computer/other digital device in the last year? How did you feel?

____

3 What do you do to keep your digital devices safe?

____

1 Complete the sentences with the verb in brackets using the present simple active, present simple passive, past simple active or past simple passive.

1 A novel or poem *is never really finished* (never really finish). You just *let* (let) it go.
2 When we .... (study) the poem in class yesterday, I .... (not understand) it.
3 It still .... (not know) exactly who .... (write) the music, but it's from the Middle Ages.
4 Whenever I .... (feel) sad, I .... (listen) to something lively by Vivaldi.
5 Last night's performance .... (take place) at the Arts Centre and .... (enjoy) by all.
6 The play .... (cancel) because the lead actor .... (break) his leg in a fall.
7 We .... (tell) to arrive on time for the rehearsal yesterday, and everyone .... (do).
8 I .... (not believe) that everyone .... (have) an artistic talent, do you?

2 Choose the best option, a, b or c.

1 a What have you been doing since we last met?
b What did you do since we've last met?
c What did you do since we've last been meeting?
2 a Have you been finishing the book yet?
b Have you finished the book yet?
c Were you finishing the book yet?
3 a We've been out together for six months.
b We've gone out together for nearly six months.
c We've been going out together for nearly six months.
4 a Did you see any good films recently?
b Have you seen any good films recently?
c Have you been seeing any good films recently?
5 a Did you work on your essay last night?
b Have you worked on your essay last night?
c Have you been working on your essay last night?
6 a Oh, no! I think I was just accidentally deleted all my photos.
b Oh, no! I think I've just been accidentally deleting all my photos.
c Oh, no! I think I've just accidentally deleted all my photos.

3 Read the sentences (1–6) and tick (✓) the correct answer, a or b.

1 *All the students in my class who studied hard went to university.*
Who went to university?
a all the students ☐
b only some of the students ☐
2 *My mum, who's a florist, works really hard.*
Why do we need commas in this sentence?
a Because if we took them away, it would mean I have more than one mum. ☐
b Because it shows that being a florist is the most important information. ☐
3 *I don't like films which have a lot of violence.*
What does this sentence mean?
a I don't like any films. ☐
b I don't like violent films. ☐
4 *I've been to Barbados, which is a Caribbean island.*
What does this sentence mean?
a There's another Barbados and it's not a Caribbean island. ☐
b I'm giving extra information about Barbados. ☐
5 *The guy ~~that~~ I spoke to at the bus stop was really friendly.*
Why don't we need a relative pronoun in this sentence?
a Because the underlined noun is the object of the verb *spoke*. ☐
b Because it's a non-defining relative clause. ☐
6 *The last question, which is easy, is this one.*
Why do we need commas in this sentence?
a To show that the part between the commas is extra information. ☐
b To show that the most important information is inside the commas. ☐

CRIME SCENE

VOCABULARY 1 >>> Talk about crimes and criminals

1 Complete the crossword with types of crime using the picture clues.

Across

2

5

7

9

Down

1

2

3

4

6

8

2 Match the sentences to the crimes in Exercise 1. Write the type of crime.

1 Be quiet! We don't want to wake the owner up. *burglary*
2 I bought this DVD copy at the market. ....
3 How many people did he kill? ....
4 I was walking down the street when a boy got a knife out and demanded my phone. ....
5 The store security guard caught him. ....
6 They want one million pounds to keep the story secret. ....
7 They have taken his son. ....
8 Look at the damage they did to the bus stop. ....
9 They used a gun to steal money from the bank. ....
10 Someone must have taken it from my bag when I was on the bus. ....

3 Complete the sentences with the correct form (noun or verb) of the words in brackets.

1 My bike *was stolen* (steal) last week from outside my house.
2 Did you see the bank .... (rob) on the news last night? The gang involved in it got away with £5 million.
3 **A:** Did you leave the lights on when we went out?
B: No, I didn't.
A: Then I think we .... (burgle). Call the police.
4 He's a serial* .... (murder) so he'll never be let out of prison.
5 .... (cybercriminal) is a growing problem these days.
6 I don't understand why people commit .... (vandalise). It's pointless.

Glossary
***serial** = several/many times

4 Complete the conversation with the words in the box.

burglary community service cybercrime fine prison sentence ~~punishment~~ vandalism

Em: So, we have to decide which crime should get which (1) *punishment* .
Lou: I think the least serious crime is (2) .... because it's against property and not people.
Em: I agree. I think it should just be a (3) .... of a few pounds. What about (4) .... – that's quite a new one?
Lou: The problem is that it can involve different things, such as stealing money or an identity. For the more serious ones I would say a (5) .... of a few years.
Em: I agree. So that leaves (6) .... Stealing things from houses is bad but if there's no violence I don't think it's so serious.
Lou: Me neither. I would say (7) .... for a few weeks.

READING

Infer meaning when you read

1 Complete the tips with the words in the box.

REMEMBER HOW TO …

infer meaning when you read

context directly indirectly sentences

- If you infer meaning in written texts, you understand what the writer doesn't express (1) ________ .
- Identify the writer's general opinion. This helps to understand individual (2) ________ .
- If you don't recognise names, use the (3) ________ to work out why they're mentioned.
- Look for idioms and other expressions that say things (4) ________ .

2 Read the text and choose the best title.

a Why people visit London
b Dangerous places in London
c Crime tours of London

Glossary
*so-called = a way to introduce a new word/phrase that might not be known

1 London is one of the most visited cities on the planet. Approximately 16 million foreign visitors come to see the sights of the city every year, and landmarks such as Big Ben and Buckingham Palace are famous throughout the world. However, it's not just these well-known sites that attract people. Surprisingly perhaps, a popular and growing attraction is the so-called* 'crime tour'. More and more companies are offering their own crime tours of the city and tourists are loving it!

2 Among the most popular of these tours are those about the life and crimes of Jack the Ripper. The fear he caused during a three-year killing spree in London's East End in the late 1880s means that nearly a century and a half later we're still talking about him. No suspect was ever found and, today, we still don't know who committed the murders in Whitechapel, but the unidentified figure has become known to all as Jack the Ripper. Choose your tour carefully as a good guide can make all the difference.

3 One of London's most famous crime landmarks is the Tower of London. Among its many ghosts is supposedly the ghost of Queen Anne Boleyn – one of Henry VIII's beheaded wives. Tours of the Tower of London help unlock the mysteries of this thousand-year-old structure. A tour guide is certainly needed to make the most of this venue.

4 One of the more disappointing crime tours is connected to the literary character of Sherlock Holmes. 221B Baker Street was the fictional home of Holmes, but the real 221B is now just a tower block of flats. The Sherlock Holmes Museum has been given the number now, even though it is arguably incorrect for its place in the street. If you love the Holmes detective stories, this is great. Otherwise, you might as well just read your favourite crime novel instead …

3 Match three people in the text to the descriptions below.

1 This person was real and we know exactly who they were. ________
2 This person did not exist. ________
3 This person was real but we don't know exactly who they were. ________

4 Choose the option that best matches the author's opinion.

1 a All Jack the Ripper tours are good.
  b Some Jack the Ripper tours are good.
  c Jack the Ripper tours are generally boring.
2 a The Tower of London tours are much better now than when they first started.
  b The Tower of London tour is usually boring.
  c Get someone to lead you around the Tower for a better experience.
3 a Only fans of Sherlock Holmes should go on the Sherlock Holmes tour.
  b The Sherlock Holmes tour is boring in general for everyone.
  c You should bring a Sherlock Holmes novel with you on the tour.

5 Read the text again and find words or phrases with the following meanings:

1 showing that something is not exact (para 1) *approximately*
2 in an unusual or unexpected way (para 1) ________
3 think about what you're doing so that nothing goes wrong or so that you avoid problems (para 2) ________
4 to have an important effect on something, especially a good effect (para 2) ________
5 used for emphasising that something is definitely true or will definitely happen (para 3) ________
6 used when stating an opinion or belief that you think can be shown to be true (para 4) ________

GO BEYOND

Find out about another crime tour in a city that interests you. Write a description of the tour and suggest it to your friends.

____
____

GRAMMAR 1 *Should, must, have to, ought to, had better*

Use modal verbs to give advice and make recommendations

1 Complete the grammar table with the words and phrases in the box.

don't/doesn't have to a good (or bad) idea have to must (x2) mustn't ought (not) to

<table>
<tr><th colspan="2">Should, must, have to, ought to, had better</th></tr>
<tr><td colspan="2">Use: For advice and recommendations.</td></tr>
<tr><td>should(n't)
(1) ....
Should you … ?</td><td>It's a good (or bad) idea.</td></tr>
<tr><td>had better (not)</td><td>It's (2) .... in a particular situation.</td></tr>
<tr><td>have/has to
(3) ....
Do you have to … ?</td><td>It's necessary, important or strongly recommended.</td></tr>
<tr><td>(4) ....</td><td>It's not necessary.</td></tr>
<tr><td>(5) ....</td><td>It's prohibited or dangerous.</td></tr>
<tr><td colspan="2">Form:
modal verb + infinitive without to</td></tr>
<tr><td colspan="2">have to or must?
■ You can often use both with the same meaning.
■ Use (6) .... when you can't choose whether or not to do something:
You have to get a licence.
■ Use (7) .... for strong recommendations:
You must visit us soon.</td></tr>
</table>

2 › Match each piece of advice (1–6) to a photo (A–F).

A 
B 
C 
D 
E 
F 

1 *You shouldn't buy them. They might not work.* ......

2 *You ought to be careful on the streets round here. There are lots of thieves around.* ......

3 *You mustn't take it. You could get in trouble with the police. Put it back.* ......

4 *They have to close the street to protect the evidence.* ......

5 *You must get the window fixed soon. It won't close.* ......

6 *You had better not use it. You might cut your hand.* ......

3 › Complete this advice for a visitor to Chicago with the verbs in the box.

had better have to (x2) must mustn't ~~should~~ shouldn't

✓ 1 I think you __should__ stay for at least three weeks.
✓ 2 You .... see the zoo and museum. I strongly recommend it!
✓ 3 You .... pack warm clothes for your holiday. It's getting cold now.
✗ 4 You don't .... worry about crime in most parts of the city.
✓ 5 You will .... get a visa to visit.
✗ 6 You .... use the 'L' railway late at night. It's better to take a taxi.
✗ 7 You .... drive on the left.

4 » Complete the conversation using *should*, *shouldn't* or *ought*.

Mia: I can't come out tonight. I (1) ought to do some work. I have an essay to hand in tomorrow.
Jessica: You (2) ________ worry so much. You're the strongest student in the class. You (3) ________ to take some time to relax.
Mia: I know, but I want to get good grades. I (4) ________ really try to get the best grades I can to make sure I get into the course I want at university. (5) ________ you be working on your essay as well?
Jessica: I (6) ________ , but I'll do it in the morning before class.
Mia: You (7) ________ do that – you always get terrible grades! I think we (8) ________ do it together.

5 » Correct the mistakes in these sentences. You must use the word *had* in all your answers.

1 It's raining. You had better to wear a coat.
It's raining. You had better wear a coat.
2 It's late. We better had take a taxi.
____
3 It's cold. I'd had better take my gloves.
____
4 We're late. We had better running.
____
5 I think we had better left now.
____
6 We had better hurrying or we'll miss the bus.
____
7 You had better joining that queue before it gets any longer.
____
8 You had to better phone your mum. She'll want to know you arrived OK.
____

6 »» Complete the sentences using the correct form of *do* + *have to*.

1 (work long hours: ✓ me ✗ wife)
I have to work long hours, but my wife doesn't have to.
2 (work when 14 years old: ✓ my grandad ✗ me)
My grandad ________
________ .
3 (buy me a present for my birthday last week: ✗ you)
____
________ – but thank you. It's lovely!
4 (work tomorrow: ✗ me)
____
________ , do I?
5 (mind the children last night: ✓ babysitter ✗ me)
The babysitter ________
________ .
6 (ask for help: ✗ you)
____
________ , did you?
7 (work very hard: ✓ me (old job) ✗ me (now))
I had ________
________ .

7 »» Match each sentence (1–8) with a response (a–h). Then complete the sentences (1–8) using *must*, *mustn't* or *don't have to*.

1 You don't have to take an umbrella. d
2 You ________ go too close to the edge of the cliff. ___
3 We ________ hurry or we'll be late. ___
4 We ________ stay together and be careful. ___
5 It ________ go in the post today. ___
6 You ________ collect me. ___
7 We ________ wait in a queue for a doctor. ___
8 You ________ report it to the police. ___

a It's dangerous.
b It isn't safe here at night.
c I can take a taxi.
d It isn't going to rain.
e I have an appointment.
f It's an important package.
g These criminals need to be found and punished.
h We don't want to be late for the party!

LISTENING

Recognise turn-taking

1 Complete the tips with the words/phrases in the box.

REMEMBER HOW TO …

recognise turn-taking

Actually Just a minute! pauses That reminds me

- (1) ______________ , *By the way*, and *Well*, change the subject.
- (2) ______________ , adds surprising information.
- *Sorry to interrupt you, but …* , and (3) ______________ are used to interrupt somebody.
- Questions and (4) ______________ invite somebody to speak.

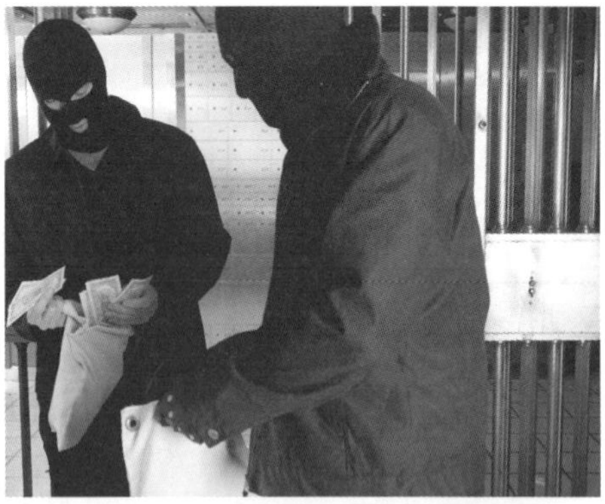

2 25 Listen to the first part of Gemma and Martin's conversation. What has just happened to them?

a They have been burgled.
b Their car has been vandalised.
c Someone is blackmailing them.

3 25 Listen again. What phrase does Gemma use to interrupt Martin?

______________ ______________ ______________ !

4 26 Listen to the next part of the conversation. Tick (✓) the things that have been taken.

clothes	☐	iPod	☐	money (€s)	☐
computer	☐	jewellery	☐	money (£s)	☐
DVD player	☐	laptop	☐	TV	☐

5 26 Listen again. Who uses these expressions, Martin or Gemma?

1 'Just a minute' Martin/Gemma
2 'Sorry to interrupt you' Martin/Gemma
3 'By the way' Martin/Gemma
4 'That reminds me' Martin/Gemma
5 'Well' Martin/Gemma

6 What punishment do you think should be given to the criminals if they are caught? ______________

Types of evidence

1 Choose the correct option to complete the sentences.

1 She was a(n) ***witness*** / ***alibi*** in the court case.
2 She gave her partner as a(n) ***witness*** / ***alibi***. He confirmed her story to the police.
3 They left no ***trail*** / ***fingerprints***. They must have been wearing gloves.
4 The knife and clothes were important ***clues*** / ***marks*** in solving the crime.
5 Once you're caught, the police will keep your ***DNA*** / ***proof*** on file.
6 The ***remains*** / ***footprints*** of some DNA were still on the clothes.
7 The ***DNA*** / ***footprints*** left clear marks in the mud.
8 There was no ***proof*** / ***mark*** and little evidence so he was free to go.
9 There were ***clues*** / ***marks*** from the car on the road after the crash.
10 The ***trail*** / ***fingerprints*** led the police to the body.

2 Complete the exchanges with the words in the box.

alibi clue DNA footprint mark proof remains witness

1 **A:** So how did they get the (1) ______ they needed to confirm their suspicions?
B: Hair found at the scene of the crime gave them the (2) ______s of the criminal.
2 **A:** They didn't have any (3) ______ to help them solve the crime.
B: No, but then a(n) (4) ______ came forward.
3 **A:** He had a(n) (5) ______ . So did he get away with it?
B: No. His shoe left a very clear (6) ______ at the crime scene.
4 **A:** The (7) ______ of breakfast were a clue.
B: Yes, but it was the black (8) ______ on the door that gave it away.

WORDS & BEYOND

3 Read the description of the film and complete it with the words and phrases in the box.

at all costs corruption crime scene in real life mafia boss prohibition punishment solve

CORRUPTED

The police have been after Andre for many years, but they cannot connect him to any crime they try to (1) ______ . Andre is the local (2) ______ who runs the town, and his (3) ______ of government officials and the police is a useful way of keeping control. One police officer, Mario, is determined to catch Andre (4) ______ , and he uses the new (5) ______ laws as a way into the gang. (6) ______ Mario is a calm, caring, family man but he turns into a brutal murderer as part of the gang. At one (7) ______ the police find Mario's DNA, but what should his (8) ______ be? Should they ignore his crime so that they can catch Andre?

4 Complete the blog comments with the words or phrases in the box.

the big screen crime keep an eye on nine-to-five job recreate turn back wander

1 ★☆☆☆☆ Who says (1) ______ doesn't pay? (2) ______ gives us yet another film where it clearly does. Not a great film and one that is trying (and failing!) to (3) ______ the atmosphere of much better mafia films. Give this one a miss – trust me …

2 ★★★★☆ (4) ______ the changes to Mario. He (5) ______s into this mafia world just at the right time, taking advantage of the prohibition laws. Policing certainly isn't a (6) ______ , but is the criminal world just too exciting for him? Can he (7) ______ time, or is his old life over? Edge-of-the-seat thriller!

5 Complete each gap in the conversation with the best word or phrase in the box.

bad press common sense in any given situation making headlines neighbourhood out of sight take precautions there's safety in numbers trouble spot valuables

Lenny: I think it's really bad that our part of town keeps (1) ______ .
Alice: It certainly gets a (2) ______ . Anyone would think that our (3) ______ is some gangland area!
Lenny: The area near the shops is a (4) ______ , but you just need to (5) ______ .
Alice: Exactly. Keep your (6) ______ (7) ______ and show some general (8) ______ and you'll be fine.
Lenny: I think that's the same (9) ______ . Also don't go there alone; (10) ______ .

GRAMMAR 2 *Can't have, could/may/might have, must have*

»»» Talk about possible explanations for things in the past

1 Complete the grammar table with the words or phrases in the box.

could evidence explanations impossible might must

Can't have, could/may/might have, must have	
Use: To talk about possible (1) .... for things in the past that are based on (2)	
(3) .... /*may*/ (4) .... *have*	You think an explanation is possible.
(5) .... *have*	You're sure an explanation is true.
can't have	You're sure an explanation is (6) ....
Form: *can't/could/must*, etc + *have* + past participle	

2 › Read the statements and choose the best option, a or b.

1 He didn't answer his phone. He must have been driving.
a I think he's driving.
b I'm sure he was driving.

2 Sorry, I might have forgotten to record it.
a I know I forgot to record it.
b I think I forgot to record it.

3 She can't have gone far.
a You're sure she hasn't gone far.
b You think she hasn't gone far.

4 I may have thrown it away.
a I think I threw it away.
b I did throw it away.

5 He could have committed the crime.
a It was him who did it.
b I think it may have been him who did it.

6 It must have been him.
a I think it was him.
b I'm sure it was him.

3 » Complete the sentences with *might have*, *must have* or *can't have*.

1 He .... locked the door. The burglars didn't need to break in.
2 It was a really busy street. Someone .... seen the murder being committed.
3 He hasn't been seen for days. People are worried he .... been kidnapped.
4 It .... been serious. He was only given a fine.
5 They .... left fingerprints. Let's check just in case.
6 Someone .... accessed my account. I haven't got any money left!
7 It .... been him – he was with me.
8 He .... left early. I can't see him anywhere.

4 »» Complete the conversation with *can't have*, *could(n't) have*, *must have* and the correct form of the verbs in the box.

be (x2) ~~be based~~ do (x2) drive jump write

Amelia: The film (1) *must have been based* on a true story. It was so realistic.
Andy: It (2) .... – we would have heard about this story before in the news or something. At the start I thought it (3) .... true as well, but now I'm sure it's not.
Amelia: I (4) .... something like that. I wouldn't have the imagination. The writer (5) .... a lot of research.
Andy: The main actor (6) .... his own stunts. It would have been too dangerous.
Amelia: I don't know. He (7) .... from the building.
Andy: Perhaps. He (8) .... the car as well. That would have been quite easy.

5 »» Write possible explanations for these situations using the prompts given. Look at the key to help you.

✓ = must have
– = could have
✗ = can't have

1 You only spent five minutes on the essay.
✗ a good job
You can't have done a good job.

2 You're here early.
✓ drive too fast
....

3 This chicken isn't cooked.
✗ cook long enough
....

4 I didn't buy that.
✓ Someone / steal my bank card
....

5 He's late.
– get lost
....

6 Those photos are online quickly.
✓ post them using his phone
....

7 He normally gets good marks; I wonder what happened.
– be ill
....

Give and react to criticism

1 Match each statement about criticism (1–4) to one of the categories (a–d).

1 Whenever someone challenges you, it makes you think differently. Criticism gives you new ways of looking at things, and new ideas. ......
2 When someone says something bad that affects you, it may mean you have things from your past that you need to deal with. ......
3 When people say something bad about us, our instinct is to fight, but generally the people around us really just want to help. ......
4 If you improve how you handle negative comments, this will save time and energy in the future. ......

a What reacting poorly to criticism suggests
b Why people give criticism
c How criticism helps us improve our skills
d Why it makes sense to learn to accept criticism

2 (27) Listen to three conversations. Match each conversation to the thing the person is being criticised for.

Conversation 1 ......
Conversation 2 ......
Conversation 3 ......

a being untidy
b getting angry
c having lost something

3 a (28) Complete the *Phrasebook* with the words in the box. Listen and check.

aggressive angry careful fault happen tired

b (28) Listen and repeat the phrases, paying attention to intonation.

4 Choose two of the situations below. Write conversations criticising someone in each situation. Try to include at least four phrases from the *Phrasebook* in each conversation.

- Your friend walks slowly and you both miss the bus.
- Your friend doesn't do much work and your group fails a class assignment.
- Your flatmate never washes the dishes.
- Your friend loses your phone.

5 Read your conversation out loud. Record it if you can and listen back to your intonation of the key phrases.

PHRASEBOOK

Criticise

You should/shouldn't have got/left ...
You could have sent/told me ...
You know/knew ...
I told you to be ...
You were too (1) .... / weren't (2) .... enough.
I'm (3) .... of ...
How could you be/leave ...
I know ... / We've all ... but ...

React to criticism

I'm sorry, ... / I know ... / Yes, ...
... but it's not my (4) ....
You're right.
It won't (5) .... again.
I shouldn't have got so (6) .... / shouted.

WRITING

Use paragraphs and topic sentences

1 Complete the tips with the words in the box.

REMEMBER HOW TO ...

use paragraphs and topic sentences

arguments opinion (x2) summarises support

- Start with an introduction. Mention your (1) ________ and what other people think.
- Write one of your (2) ________ in each of the following paragraphs.
- Introduce a topic sentence in each paragraph that (3) ________ its argument.
- Include other sentences to (4) ________ or explain the topic sentence.
- End with a conclusion. State your (5) ________ again and summarise your main argument.

2 Read the essay and choose the main topic.

a The rise of crime
b Solving youth crime
c Prisons and youth crime

Most people would agree that if a certain type of behaviour becomes normal for someone when they are young, then it will continue for a long time. Therefore, there are concerns in many places where levels of youth crime are increasing rapidly. There are arguably a number of causes of this youth crime issue, and dealing with those causes should help to solve the problem.

(1) ___ These can range from divorce of the parents to hard economic times. One thing that tends to be common to most cases is that there is a sudden or big change in an otherwise stable environment. Therefore, providing systems of social support young people can use is vital.

(2) ___ When more than 50% of people under 25 are unemployed, despite many having a good education, it is understandable that some may look to other methods of earning money. Providing training schemes or government work may be a solution.

(3) ___ This is perhaps also connected to the family and work issues mentioned above. Giving young people safe environments such as youth clubs may help keep them out of trouble.

In conclusion, youth crime is connected to many wider factors in society. Family circumstances, friendship groups and employment opportunities are all key to preventing people from following this path.

3 Write the letter of each topic sentence (a–c) in the correct place (1–3) in the essay.

a Furthermore, youth unemployment arguably leads to increased crime levels among young people.
b Lastly, young people can be easily influenced by their peers. In some extreme cases this can lead to people joining gangs.
c Statistics* show that many young offenders – people who commit crimes – often come from families which have other issues affecting them as well.

Glossary
***Statistics** = a group of numbers that represent facts or that describe a situation

4 a Number these sentences in the correct order to form a new paragraph.

___ a Low family income, long-term unemployment or having one or more parents who were themselves criminals is another major factor.
___ b Identifying such families and providing social and financial support is key.
___ c In some cases, however, it isn't a sudden change but simply poor role models in the home that's to blame.

b Look back at the essay in Exercise 2. Where would you insert the new paragraph?

After the (first/second/third/fourth ...) ________ paragraph.

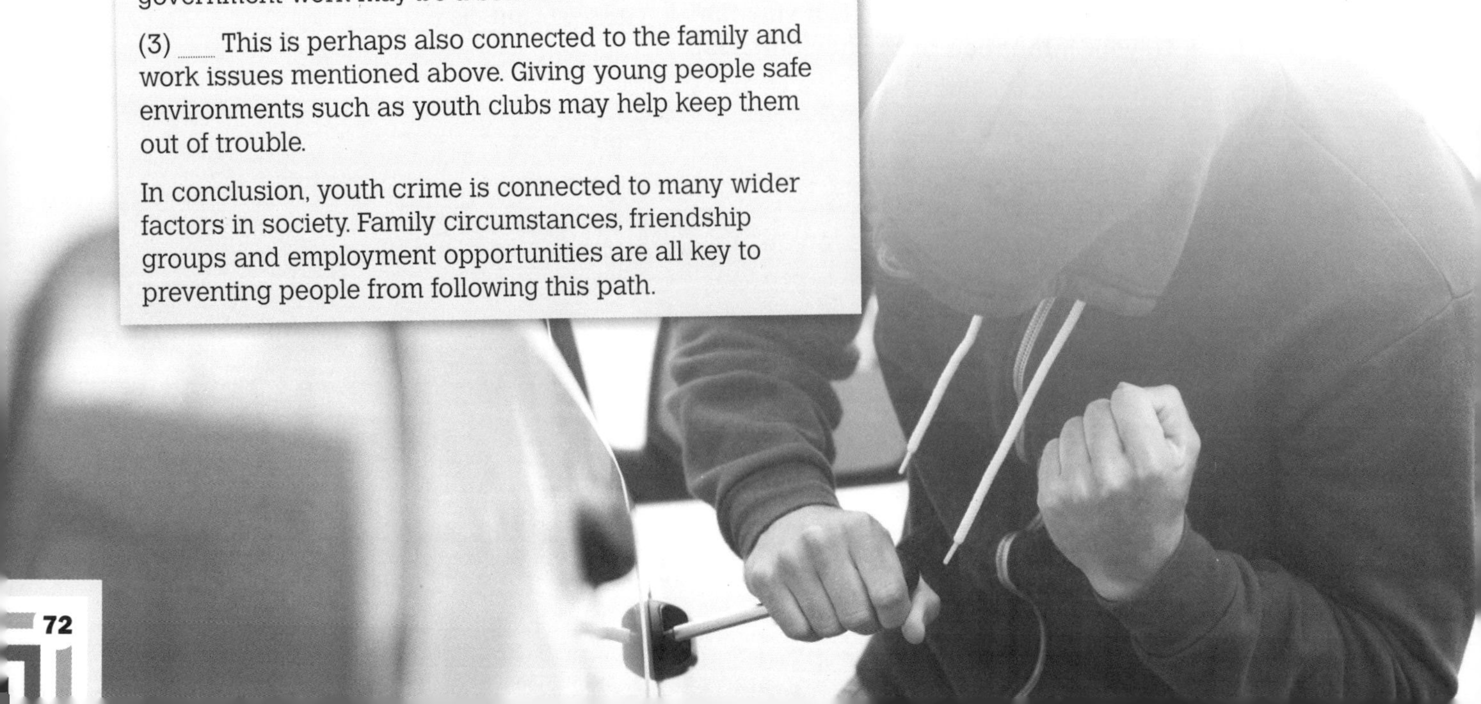

WRITING PLAN

5 You're going to write an essay on the following topic. Use the *Writing plan* to help you prepare.

Why do many criminals commit crimes again after leaving prison and what can be done to change this?

WRITING PLAN

Make notes for your essay.

1 Introduction. My opinion ______ ☐

2 Main body. Arguments
  1 ______ ☐
  2 ______ ☐
  3 ______ ☐

3 Conclusion ______ ☐

WRITE AND CHECK

6 Write your essay. Then tick (✓) the stages in the *Writing plan*.

Take responsibility for your actions

1 Read the statements (1–6) and decide if they relate to A or B below.

A = reasons why taking responsibility for your actions is difficult
B = ways to take responsibility for your actions

1 People can lack confidence in their own abilities and have feelings of low self-esteem. ______
2 Understand that you cannot place the blame on others for the choices you make. ______
3 People develop arrogance (overconfidence). They feel they must act like they are better than other people. ______
4 It's OK to make mistakes. No-one will think less of you. ______
5 Some people are on their guard because they think others treat them unfairly. ______
6 Learn ways to let go of fear. Fear can create insecurities. ______

2 a Read about Maria's situation. What won't she take responsibility for, and why? ______

Maria's got a group presentation to do. She knows she's the best presenter in the group, so she isn't worried or stressed. The other members of her group have been meeting regularly to prepare and practise and have become quite annoyed with her laziness. She thinks they need to calm down as it only counts for 20% of their course mark anyway. After the presentation the teacher surprises them by allowing the group members to mark each other. Her group all give her an F and she fails. Maria complains to the teacher but he refuses to change her mark. She blames the group and thinks they are just jealous of her speaking skills.

b What advice would you give Maria? ______

c Do you think her teacher's decision was right? Why?/Why not? ______

KNOW YOURSELF

1 Complete the sentences from film reviews with the words in the box. Use the clue in brackets after each sentence to help you.

average controversial dull elaborate moving powerful quirky stunning subtle unique

1 'A(n) ______ drama that will make anyone cry.' (causing strong feelings of sadness or sympathy)
2 'Incredibly ______ ! I nearly fell asleep.' (not interesting or exciting in any way)
3 'Just another comedy romance – a very ______ movie.' (typical and usual)
4 '______ ! Nothing quite like it!' (the only one of its type)
5 'The humour is clever and very ______ .' (not obvious)
6 'A(n) ______ story that's sure to get people talking.' (something people disagree with or don't approve of)
7 'The story is too ______ and difficult to follow.' (very detailed and complicated)
8 'A(n) ______ story. Not for everyone.' (slightly strange)
9 '______ visual effects.' (very impressive or beautiful)
10 'A(n) ______ story that will get people thinking.' (influence or control what people think)

2 Put the phrases in the correct categories.

apart from as a rule by and large except for the exception generally on the whole

talking about the general situation

talking about differences

3 Complete the newspaper headlines with the words in the box.

ash buries deaths destroys disaster homelessness lava rescues spreads strikes survivors war

1 COASTGUARD ______ OVER TWENTY ______ FROM COLLAPSED BOAT

2 VOLCANO COVERS TOWN IN ______ AS ______ FLOWS DOWN MOUNTAIN

3 ______ ______ AS UNEMPLOYMENT RISES

4 HURRICANE ______ COAST AND ______ HUNDREDS OF HOMES

5 ______ AS AVALANCHE ______ TOWN UNDER 20 FEET OF SNOW

6 ______ LEADS TO 2,000 ______

ALL ABOUT ME

1 What films have you seen recently that were good?

______

2 How would you describe them?

______

3 What's the worst film you've ever seen? Why?

______

1 Complete the sentences with *can't have, could have* or *must have* and a question tag.

1 He *can't have* finished it already, *can he*? I've still got lots to do.
2 She ______ been breaking the speed limit, ______? You can't get here that quickly.
3 You ______ left your wallet at home, ______? Hopefully we'll find it later.
4 They ______ got lost, ______? They're really late.
5 **A:** We ______ missed it, ______? **B:** No, we're early ... don't worry.
6 He ______ phoned while we were out, ______? Maybe that's why he hasn't arrived.

2 Complete the conversation with the infinitive or *-ing* form of the verbs in the box.

arrive beat break hold move shake stand try

Zainab: I saw a man (1) ______ into a house the other day.
Tim: What did you do?
Zainab: After he'd gone inside, I crept to the window and saw him (2) ______ a bag with valuable things in it. I phoned the police, but I was really nervous. I could feel my hands (3) ______ .
Tim: Did you wait for the police?
Zainab: I did. I saw them (4) ______ and get out of their car, but then I left. I didn't want the man to see me (5) ______ there.
Tim: I heard someone (6) ______ to break into my house the other week.
Zainab: Did you feel scared?
Tim: I felt nervous. I could hear my heart (7) ______ really fast. I decided the best thing to do was to make a lot of noise. When he heard me (8) ______ around the house, he ran away.

3 Look at the pairs of sentences. Match each sentence (a and b) to its meaning (i or ii).

1
a Claire's working hard. — i Claire's a hard worker.
b Claire works hard. — ii Claire's doing a lot of work at the moment.
2
a I lived in Madrid for three years. — i I used to live in Madrid.
b I've been living in Madrid for three years. — ii I live in Madrid today.
3
a We've been friends for ages. — i We're friends now.
b We were friends for ages. — ii We aren't friends now.
4
a I got up, had breakfast and then had a shower. — i I had a shower before breakfast.
b I got up and, when I'd had a shower, I had breakfast. — ii I had a shower after breakfast.
5
a I was reading the paper at 10.30. — i I was in the middle of reading the paper at 10.30.
b I had read the paper by 10.30. — ii I was no longer reading the paper at 10.30.
6
a I've seen the carnival several times before. — i I still watch the carnival.
b I saw the carnival several times as a child. — ii I no longer watch the carnival.
7
a We're having lunch at 1 o'clock. — i We do this every day.
b We have lunch at 1 o'clock. — ii This is what we are doing today.
8
a I've been working on this project for a month. — i The project's a lot of work!
b I've worked on this project for a month. — ii This is how long the project has taken me.

4 Match the sentence halves. Join them with *which*.

1 My phone is broken. *e* — a That was nice of them.
2 My parents paid for the meal. ___ — b It caused a traffic jam.
3 The police closed the road. ___ — c That was careless of you.
4 You left your phone on my desk. ___ — d That upset her.
5 Karen didn't get the job. ___ — e It's really annoying.
6 You left the door open. ___ — f That made it cold in here.

1 *My phone is broken, which is really annoying.*
2 ______
3 ______
4 ______
5 ______
6 ______

UNIT 7

TURNING POINTS

VOCABULARY 1 »» Talk about money

1 a Read the clues and complete the words. Then check your answers by finding them in the word search.

1 m ___ ___ ___ ___ (get money by doing something)
2 w ___ ___ ___ ___ ___ (use money when it's not necessary)
3 s ___ ___ ___ ___ ___ (use money to buy something)
4 e ___ ___ ___ ___ (get money by working)
5 b ___ ___ ___ ___ ___ ___ (be given money for a time from somebody with permission)
6 p ___ ___ ___ (give money because you've bought something)
7 i ___ ___ ___ ___ ___ ___ ___ (receive money because of someone's death)
8 r ___ ___ ___ ___ ___ (collect money for a particular purpose)
9 d ___ ___ ___ ___ ___ (give money to a charity)
10 o ___ ___ ___ (have to give money back to someone in the future)
11 w ___ ___ ___ ___ ___ ___ ___ (take money from your bank account)

X	W	W	P	O	E	O	E	X	F
X	I	B	O	K	G	M	S	D	T
E	T	I	A	R	O	Y	I	I	T
T	H	M	N	N	R	J	A	X	G
A	D	Y	E	H	E	O	R	W	E
N	R	Y	A	A	E	A	B	L	T
O	A	O	G	P	S	R	R	R	S
D	W	S	P	E	N	D	I	N	A
Z	O	W	E	X	H	P	R	T	W
C	L	I	D	Y	H	W	L	H	Z

b Draw an arrow next to each verb above to show if it relates to money coming in to you (‹) or money leaving you (›).

2 a Complete each statement with the correct form of a verb from Exercise 1.

1 *You don't think I could ______ some money from you until the end of the month, do you?*

2 *I'm really grateful. I've just ______ money from an uncle I only met a few times.*

3 *I tried to ______ some cash, but I put in the wrong PIN and the machine ate my card.*

4 *We're making and selling cakes to ______ money for our school trip to Italy.*

5 *Don't you think that buying new clothes every season is just ______ money?*

6 *She could have ______ up to $100,000 a year if she'd got the job in New York.*

7 *I'm giving you €50 for your birthday, but don't ______ it all at once.*

8 *We didn't have to ______ anything to get in as it was a free concert.*

9 *In some cultures you're supposed to ______ 10% of your salary to charity.*

b Complete the sentence with the missing word.

If I borrow money from you, you l ___ ___ ___ me money.

3 Complete the text with the words in the box.

account allowance cash debt income savings

I've never had any (1) ______ in a bank and no bank will let me open a(n) (2) ______ now because I'm homeless and don't have a regular (3) ______ . My parents threw me out last year and won't give me a(n) (4) ______ . I hate to get into (5) ______ as I never know when or if I can pay someone back, so I never borrow. However, I do get a bit of (6) ______ by playing music in the streets. Do you want to hear a song?

4 Complete the text using the correct form of the words in brackets.

The business was very (1) *profitable* (profit) last year and what they've paid me – my (2) ______ (earn) – has gone up by 20%. With the (3) ______ (inherit) money from my grandfather, we'll be able to afford the expensive school (4) ______ (fee) of Merton Private Boys School and Josh will get the best education money can buy. I'll go to the bank and make a (5) ______ (withdraw) in order to make a (6) ______ (donate) to the hospital that looked after Grandfather so well in his last few months of life.

5 a These are some lines from different songs. Guess what the last word of each sentence is.

1 Money makes the world go ______ .
2 Money can't buy you ______ .
3 Money, money, money must be funny in the rich man's ______ .
4 If I were a wealthy man … I wouldn't have to work ______ .
5 It's not about the money, money, ______ .

b Now check to see if you were right by looking at the answers in the box below.

1 round 2 love 3 world 4 hard 5 money

Make notes for a summary

1 Complete the tips with the words in the box.

REMEMBER HOW TO …

make notes for a summary

details	information	quote	whole

- Read the (1) .... text and note important (2) ....
- Read again and add any interesting (3) .... to your notes.
- Copy a (4) .... if it's important.

2 Read the text and choose the best title.

a Money for nothing
b If you don't ask, you don't get
c Who needs money?

BLOG

HOME ABOUT CONTACT

1 Hi. I'm Lara. If you'd been in downtown New York 15 years ago, you might well have seen me in the street, but you wouldn't have recognised me. Back then I was over two metres tall and I used to stand completely still for up to six hours at a time. Let me explain … I was a living statue. I painted my face and stood on a box wearing a long dress that went down to the ground. I put a hat in front of me and if people wanted to, they could put some money in it. If they did, I'd offer them a flower. If they didn't, I'd look at them sadly and slowly wave goodbye.

2 I did this for five years and what did I learn? Well, firstly, that (1) I could make people uncomfortable. Some shouted at me: 'Get a job!' And others walked past quickly without looking at me at all. But if someone stopped, I looked into their eyes and sometimes I could see that their eyes said: 'Nobody really sees me.' By the way, (2) I did make enough money to live doing this – usually between \$60 and \$100 a day. But the main thing I discovered was that (3) if you ask for something and make a connection with people – even strangers, even silently and just standing still, some of them are willing to give.

3 Now I'm a musician and I give away my music free online. Well, how many people actually buy music these days? But making music costs money, so I had the radical idea of asking on the internet through a crowdsourcing* site if anybody out there would like to donate to help me make my next record. Twenty thousand people did and I raised over \$1,000,000! Just by asking …

Glossary
***crowdsourcing** = asking the online community to donate services, knowledge, ideas or money

3 a Now close the book and note down five important things you remember from the text. When you've finished, open your book again.

b Rewrite your notes here. But first check them against the text to make sure the information is correct.

1 ....
2 ....
3 ....
4 ....
5 ....

4 Read the first paragraph again and tick (✓) the most important piece of information. (Tick one box only.)

1 She lived in New York 15 years ago. ☐
2 She used to be over two metres tall. ☐
3 She was a living statue. ☐
4 She painted her face. ☐
5 She put a hat in front of her. ☐
6 She gave people flowers. ☐

5 Read the second paragraph of the text again and decide if the underlined parts give important information (*I*) or interesting details (*D*).

1 ...... 2 ...... 3 ......

6 Read the last paragraph of the text again and tick (✓) the most important point. (Tick one box only.)

1 Not many people buy music online these days. ☐
2 She earned a lot of money. ☐
3 She's a musician now, not a living statue. ☐
4 She had an idea to raise money. ☐

GO BEYOND

Use the internet to find out more about crowdsourcing. Find out:

- what it is.
- when it started.
- how it works.

GRAMMAR 1 Conditionals review

Talk about possible or imaginary situations in the present and future

1 Complete the grammar table with the words and phrases in the box.

always true   future (x2)   imaginary situations
past simple   possible situations   present simple (x2)

Conditionals review
In conditional sentences an *if*-clause describes a situation, and a second clause describes its results.
Zero conditional
Use: To talk about situations that are (1) ………… .
Form: *If* + (2) ………… , … present simple
First conditional
Use: To talk about (3) ………… in the (4) ………… and their results.
Form: *If* + (5) ………… , … *will/may/might* + infinitive without *to*
Second conditional
Use: To talk about unlikely or (6) ………… in the present or (7) ………… and their results.
Form: *If* + (8) ………… , … *would/wouldn't* + infinitive without *to*

2 Read the statements and choose the correct answer, *Yes* or *No*.

1 If you don't have money, you can't buy things.
   a Is this about a future situation? Yes/No
   b Is this about something that is generally true? Yes/No
2 If I won a lot of money, I would donate some to charity.
   a Have I won a lot of money? Yes/No
   b Will I donate money to charity now? Yes/No
3 If I get paid, I'll take you for dinner.
   a Is this about the future? Yes/No
   b Have I been paid? Yes/No

3 › Match the sentence halves.

1 If you don't make mistakes,
2 If you can't be good,
3 If a thing's worth doing,
4 If you don't like the heat,
5 If you want peace,
6 If you play with fire,
7 If at first you don't succeed,
8 If the shoe fits,
9 If anything can go wrong,
10 If you want a thing done well,

a get out of the kitchen.
b wear it.
c you don't make anything.
d it will.
e be careful.
f try, try, try again.
g it's worth doing well.
h you must prepare for war.
i do it yourself.
j you get burned.

4 › Choose the correct options to complete the text below.

Perhaps if it wasn't so cold, I (1) ***didn't*** / ***wouldn't*** mind it so much. But if you've got nowhere to stay in weather like this, it (2) ***can*** / ***could*** be really hard to keep warm. If I had family here, I suppose they (3) ***will*** / ***would*** take me in for a while, but I don't and, of course, I don't have any money to get back to my country. If I (4) ***do*** / ***did***, I'd certainly go. I had hoped things would be better here, but at least I know I can get a hot meal once a day if I (5) ***went*** / ***go*** to the Red Cross centre.
Anyway – time to move on. It's getting dark. If I don't find a nice shop doorway soon, there (6) ***aren't*** / ***won't be*** any left.

5 a ›› Rearrange the words to make questions.

1 you / do / if / asked you / in the street / would / a stranger / for some money / what / ?
What would you do if a stranger asked you for some money in the street?

2 unexpectedly / you / 1,000 euros / what / you / won / do / would / if / ?
....

3 money / asked / they / you / would / to friends / lend / if / you / ?
....

4 charity / donate to / if / would / money to spare / you had / you / which / ?
....

5 enough money in your account, / if / buy it / your credit card / you / you / have / don't / using / can / ?
....

6 people / can / live / more cheaply / not a town / if / they / live in a village / ?
....

7 change / very rich, / might / were / you / if / how / your life / ?
....

b Match the questions in Exercise 5a to the answers below.

..... a The WWF – World Wide Fund for Nature – to help save animals.
..... b I don't think it would much, actually.
..... c Not unless they signed a note promising to pay it back.
..... d I'd give them some change if I had a little in my pocket.
..... e I think I'd probably save it.
..... f I don't think that's a good idea as I don't want to get into debt.
..... g If they grow their own food, I expect so.

6 ››› Complete the second sentence so that it has a similar meaning to the first. Use between four and six words including the word given in brackets. Do not change the word given. Contractions (*don't, won't*) count as two words.

1 I don't have my card, so I can't make a withdrawal.
(could) If I *had my card*, *I could* get some cash out.

2 I'm not rich, so I don't go on foreign holidays.
(were) If I ...., ... travel abroad.

3 I can always let you borrow money when you need it.
(lend) If you ...., ... you some any time.

4 Why don't you ask your mum for more pocket money?
(would) If you ...., ... she give you more pocket money?

5 My advice is to put the money in another bank.
(were) If ...., ... change banks.

6 I won't book for the theatre because the tickets are too expensive.
(cheaper) If the tickets ...., ... get some.

7 I need to hurry so I can watch *Rich and Famous* on TV.
(won't) If I ...., ... be able to watch *Rich and Famous* on TV.

LISTENING

Predict what a story will be about

1 Complete the tips with the words and phrases in the box.

REMEMBER HOW TO ...

predict what a story will be about

consequences   events   scene   typical information   visual clues

- Look at any pictures or (1) ______________ .
- Think about (2) ______________ in a story:
  - Setting the (3) ______________ . (Where and when did the story happen? Who was involved?)
  - Describing (4) ______________ . (What happened? How did the speaker feel?)
  - Talking about (5) ______________ . (What was the result?)

2 Look at the pictures and think about what story they might tell. Predict the story and number the pictures in a logical order, from 1 to 5.

A ☐

B ☐

C ☐

D ☐

E ☐

3 ▶29 Listen to the story and check your predictions from Exercise 2. Write the correct order of the pictures below.

1 Picture: ____
2 Picture: ____
3 Picture: ____
4 Picture: ____
5 Picture: ____

4 ▶29 Listen again and decide whether these statements are true (*T*) or false (*F*).

1 Waris spent her childhood in a city. T/F
2 Waris got married at a young age. T/F
3 Waris's uncle introduced her to a photographer. T/F
4 Waris worked internationally. T/F
5 Waris became rich. T/F
6 Waris achieved success in more than one type of work. T/F

5 What do you think Waris might do next? Tick (✓) one box.

1 Start modelling again after her 50th birthday. ☐
2 Stop working for the United Nations. ☐
3 Give up all work and retire a wealthy woman. ☐

6 Do some research to find out about what Waris Dirie is doing now. Make notes.

____

____

____

VOCABULARY 2

Adjectives ending with *-ful* and *-less*

1 a Draw emoticons next to the adjectives to show whether they have a positive meaning ☺, negative meaning ☹, or are neutral 😐.

1 stressful ......
2 hopeless ......
3 forgetful ......
4 careful ......
5 motionless ......
6 pointless ......
7 grateful ......
8 helpless ......
9 careless ......
10 peaceful ......

b Which three adjectives in Exercise 1a which end in *-less* can change their ending to *-ful*?

1 ....
2 ....
3 ....

2 Choose the correct option to complete the sentences.

1 I felt so ***helpless*** / ***pointless*** just watching, but there was nothing I could do to make the situation better.
2 If you're not ***careful*** / ***careless***, you can spend all your allowance before you know it.
3 My sister's ***forgetful*** / ***hopeless*** at saving money – she spends it as soon as she gets it.
4 We're all really ***peaceful*** / ***grateful*** for all the work you've done on this – thanks a million.
5 I don't think working in a bank is a very ***motionless*** / ***stressful*** job, do you?

3 Complete each exchange with the words in the box.

careless forgetful grateful hopeless motionless peaceful pointless stressful

1 **A:** Wasn't it pretty (1) .... spending four years at university just to find yourself unemployed afterwards?
B: No. I'm (2) .... for the experience and things aren't totally (3) .... I'm planning to start my own little business.

2 **A:** Isn't it lovely and (4) .... here?
B: Indeed. Such a change from the busy, (5) .... life we lead in the city.

3 **A:** Uncle Pete's such a (6) .... driver. He's had two accidents in the last month.
B: Yes, I think it's his age. He's also becoming (7) .... Yesterday he didn't know where he'd parked the car. I saw him standing (8) .... in the middle of the street with his eyes closed trying to remember.

4 Write three adjectives from Exercise 1a to describe the man in the photo and/or the situation. Share your answers in your next English lesson.

1 .... 2 .... 3 ....

WORDS & BEYOND

5 Complete the sentences with the words in the box.

cardboard convertible junction parcel radical saying

1 I have to go to the post office to pick up a ....
2 What do you think the old .... 'money makes money' means?
3 What I like about my .... is that you can feel the wind blowing through your hair as you drive along.
4 If you're sleeping on the streets, you can use a .... box to stay warm.
5 It was a .... idea at the time that everybody should get free healthcare and education.
6 That street .... is really dangerous. There are always accidents happening there.

6 Complete the words with the correct letters.

Shak: Hey, good to see you, (1) *d* _ _ *e*. It's been a while. So, how's it going?
Dwayne: Oh, man. You know – Life's really not (2) *f* _ _ _ at the moment. Too much heavy stuff to deal with.
Shak: Come on, brother; it can't be all bad. Tell you what – I'm having a party and a (3) *s* _ _ _ _ _ _ _ *r* at my place tonight. It's just a (4) *b* _ _ *k* or so away from where you live, that right? Come along.
Dwayne: Really? Wow!
Shak: Yeah – and no parents. So, no excuses! See you after nine – I'll text you the address. I've got the (5) *g* _ _ _ *s* – you know, the party food and drink – so you don't need to bring anything along.

GRAMMAR 2 Third conditional

»» Talk about imaginary situations in the past

1 Complete the grammar table with the words and phrases in the box.

have if might participle past perfect would wouldn't

Third conditional
Use: To talk about imaginary situations in the (1) .... and their results.
Form: **Positive and negative** *If* + past (2) ...., + *would(n't) have* + past (3) ..../perfect ...
Questions *Would* + subject + (4) .... + past participle (+ (5) .... + past perfect)? *Would you have been late (if you hadn't driven)?*
Short answers *Yes, I* (6) .... / *No, I* (7) ....
Note You can also use *should*, *could* and (8) .... in the result clause. If the sentence begins with *If*, put a comma before the second clause. Don't use a comma if the *if*-clause is the second one.

2 › Read the statements and choose the correct answer.

1 If I'd sold my house last year, I would have been able to get a new car.
   a Did I sell my house last year? Yes/No
   b Did I buy a new car? Yes/No
2 Jane could have bought a new car if she'd saved instead of spending.
   a Did Jane buy a new car? Yes/No
   b Did Jane spend most of her money? Yes/No
3 Nobody would have believed us if we hadn't taken a photo of the event.
   a Did anybody believe us? Yes/No
   b Did we take a photo of the event? Yes/No
4 Joe wouldn't have left his old job if he hadn't had another one to go to.
   a Did Joe leave his old job? Yes/No
   b Did Joe have another job to go to? Yes/No
5 If I'd been more careful, I wouldn't have broken the bowl.
   a Was I careful? Yes/No
   b Did I break the bowl? Yes/No
6 If I hadn't been in such a hurry, I wouldn't have left my mobile at home.
   a Was I in a hurry? Yes/No
   b Did I bring my mobile phone with me? Yes/No

3 »› Choose the correct option to complete the sentences.

1 If I ***didn't*** / ***hadn't*** had a cold, I ***would have*** / ***had*** gone with her.
2 If I ***had known*** / ***knew*** about the problem earlier, I ***could*** / ***could have*** fixed it.
3 I wouldn't ***had*** / ***have*** called you in the middle of the night if it ***wouldn't*** / ***hadn't*** been an emergency.

4 »› Rearrange the words in *italics* to make third conditional sentences. Start with the words in bold.

1 Kate: *me, / have / told /* ***If you*** */ had / would / I / understood / .*
....
2 Will: *forgiven /* **Would** */ me / if / you / have / had / sorry / said / I / ?*
....
3 Freda: *thought about the consequences / it / if /* ***Would*** */ still done / have / you / had / you / ?*
....
4 Liam: ***I*** */ have / if / might not / Tom / done it / hadn't encouraged me / .*
....
5 Kim: *you / arrived, / it / been a disaster / would / hadn't /* ***If*** */ have / .*
....
6 Li: go on without / **Wouldn't** / have / able to / you / been / me / ?
....

5 »»› Use the information about George to write sentences using the third conditional.

1 George was unemployed so he didn't have an income.
   If George *hadn't been unemployed, he would have had* an income.
2 He had free time so he decided to work as a volunteer for a charity.
   If he .... able to volunteer for a charity.
3 He met Anne because she also worked for the same charity.
   If Anne .... her.
4 He married Anne because she was rich.
   He .... rich.
5 She realised he didn't love her so she divorced him.
   She .... he didn't love her.
6 George was alone because he didn't marry for the right reason.
   George .... for the wrong reason.

SPEAKING

Send letters and parcels at the post office

1 (30) **Listen to three conversations. What do the people want to send and where do they want to send it? Choose the correct options.**

	item	destination
Conversation 1	parcel / letter / money	France / China / Croatia
Conversation 2	parcel / letter / money	France / China / Croatia
Conversation 3	parcel / letter / money	France / China / Croatia

2 Complete the *Phrasebook* with the words in the box.

cheaper cost long much need options pay send stamp

3 (30) **Look at the table below. Listen to the conversations again and tick (✓) the correct columns.**

	1	2	3
The customer asks about the cost/price.	✓		
The customer asks about alternatives.			
The customer asks when their post will arrive.			

4 (30) **Listen to the conversations again and complete them with the phrases you hear. Write exactly what you hear.**

Conversation 1

Rav: Good morning. (1) .... if that's possible.
Assistant: No problem Sir, as long as you have the account details and your ID with you.
Rav: I have my driving licence. Will that do?
Assistant: That's fine. So, if you'd just fill out this form.
Rav: Oh, (2) .... – like a transfer fee?
Assistant: I'm afraid we do charge a €10 fee for this service, yes.
Rav: I see. Er … (3) .... ?
Assistant: Well, you could write a cheque and put it in the post. That would cost you just the price of a stamp.

Conversation 2

Vlad: Hello, (4) ....
Assistant: Right. Well, I'll just weigh it for you … Do you want to send it express? It's just over three kilos, so that would be £12.52.
Vlad: Oh, that's more than I expected. (5) .... ?
Assistant: Of course. We can send it standard parcel rate.
Vlad: Um. (6) .... with the standard rate?
Assistant: It should be there within a week.
Vlad: That's fine. It's not urgent. (7) .... ?

Conversation 3

Mira: Hi. (8) .... ? It's going to France.
Assistant: OK. Here you are. That's 80p.
Mira: So, (9) .... ? It is airmail, isn't it? Only it's a job application and needs to get there as fast as possible.
Assistant: With first class, it should arrive tomorrow.

5 (31) **Listen and repeat the phrases, paying special attention to stress and intonation.**

PHRASEBOOK

Explaining what you want

I'd like a (1) .... to send a letter to Poland, please.

I (2) .... to send this parcel to Uruguay.

I'd like to (3) .... some money to someone in Japan.

Asking for information

Can you tell me how (4) .... it would cost?

How much will it (5) .... ?

Is there a (6) .... way to send it?

How (7) .... will it take to get there?

Are there any other (8) .... ?

Do I have to (9) .... anything extra?

6 a Write a conversation between a customer and an assistant at a post office. Explain what you want and ask for information about the price, the alternatives and the expected delivery date.

A: ....
....
B: ....
....
A: ....
....
B: ....
....
A: ....
....
B: ....
....

b Read your conversation aloud, paying special attention to the key phrases. Record yourself if you can.

WRITING

Use persuasive language

1 Complete the tips with the words in the box.

REMEMBER HOW TO ...

use persuasive language

action address directly donate identify imperatives second third

- Use (1) __________ with action words like *help*, (2) __________ and *give*.
- Use (3) __________ conditionals to make people (4) __________ with the situation.
- Use 'you' to (5) __________ the reader (6) __________.
- Use first and (7) __________ conditionals to describe how a(n) (8) __________ will help or helped in the past.

2 Complete the text with the words in the box.

food forest lake people village wind

3 What does the advertisement say you can do on the holiday? Choose the correct answers.

1 meet people Yes/No
2 do water sports Yes/No
3 climb mountains Yes/No
4 learn how to cook local dishes Yes/No
5 see wild animals Yes/No
6 listen to the sounds of nature Yes/No

4 Read the text again and answer the questions.

1 Which verbs are used as imperatives?

__________ __________ __________

2 How many times is 'you' used? __________

3 Which paragraph uses:
 a the first conditional? paragraph ____
 b the second conditional? paragraph ____
 c the third conditional? paragraph ____

4 Which adjectives are used? Find and write nine.

__________ __________ __________
__________ __________ __________
__________ __________ __________

5 How many questions are asked? __________

Break into NATURE

1 Imagine wild beauty. How would you feel if you were surrounded by stunning scenery – walking through natural (1) __________s and swimming in cool mountain (2) __________s? You hear nothing but the sounds of the birds in the trees, the light (3) __________ moving the leaves and the river running by. As the sun goes down, you see the lights of the traditional (4) __________ ahead and look forward to an evening with friendly (5) __________ and delicious local (6) __________ and drinks.

2 You'll be amazed at what a nature break can do for you. And if you want to go horse-riding, rafting or kayaking, we'll arrange it. Here's what one of our guests wrote: 'If I hadn't come on this holiday, I would have just stayed in the city and missed one of the best times of my life.'

SO, WHAT ARE YOU WAITING FOR? CONTACT US AT WWW.BREAKINTONATURE.IS AND SEE WHAT A DIFFERENCE A BREAK INTO NATURE CAN MAKE.

WRITING PLAN

5 You're going to write an advertisement for a holiday company. Use the *Writing plan* to help you prepare.

WRITING PLAN

Make notes for your advertisement.

1 What type of holiday are you offering? (eg beach, adventure, cultural, winter and nature) ☐

2 What can people do on this holiday? (eg relax, try something new, be educated, discover new places) ☐

3 Who might be interested in this type of holiday? (eg children, teens, singles, couples, older people) ☐

4 Why should people choose your holiday? (eg it's different, recommended by others, cheap) ☐

5 What questions will you ask in the advertisement? ☐

6 Which adjectives will you use? ☐

7 Which imperatives will you use? ☐

8 Which conditionals will you try to use? ☐

WRITE AND CHECK

6 Write your advertisement. Then tick (✓) the stages in the *Writing plan*.

Adapt to changing situations

1 Read these sayings. Write what each one means in your own words. Which one do you agree with more?

1 A leopard can't change its spots.

2 A change is as good as a rest.

2 What does the following statement mean?

'*You cannot step twice into the same river.*' (Heraclitus)

3 Read the exchanges and decide if what the people say shows flexibility (✓) or not (✗).

1 **Kyle:** How about playing on Saturday this week?
Jay: But we always play on Fridays. ☐

2 **Ona:** Sorry about being late. We've missed the start.
Jim: Let's get a coffee. We can use the tickets for the late show. ☐

3 **Andi:** I've won a flight for a weekend in Barcelona and I can take a friend. That's you, by the way.
Loti: You know I always have my hair done on Saturdays. Can't it be during the week? ☐

4 **Wan:** Over the last three years, my salary has gone down by 30%.
Alf: So has mine. That's why I don't eat meat anymore. It's too expensive. ☐

4 Rearrange the words to complete the advice.

1 can / change / you / Change / what / .

2 can't / Accept / what / change / you / .

3 difference / the / Know / .

COMMUNICATE & COOPERATE

1 Complete the paragraph with the words in the box.

crossroads eye junctions local sense situation spots traffic

The basic rule about driving is simple: don't hit anything and don't let anything hit you. It's common (1) .... , isn't it? In any given (2) .... , that's what you have to remember. Keep an (3) .... on what's going on behind you as well as in front of you and be particularly careful at (4) .... , especially (5) .... If you're driving in your (6) .... area, you'll know where the trouble (7) .... are, so avoid them if you can. And if you're stuck in (8) .... , keep calm. Sounding your horn doesn't make the car ahead go any faster.

2 Choose the correct options to complete the conversation.

Vlad

Igor

Igor: For the video shoot, I'm a (1) ***zombie*** / ***dystopia***, you know – one of the living dead.

Vlad: Yeah. Well, you won't need any make-up.

Igor: I've got to be (2) ***terrifying*** / ***erupting*** so people are really (3) ***scary*** / ***scared*** of me.

Vlad: You're (4) ***realistic*** / ***creepy*** enough in real (5) ***time*** / ***life***.

Igor: But how should I speak? Should I (6) ***slam*** / ***groan*** as if in deep pain or (7) ***scream*** / ***whisper*** loudly at the top of my voice?

Vlad: None of this matters. Listen carefully: When it's over I will (8) ***remain*** / ***bury*** you after sucking all the blood out of you and then you will wake up like me and you'll be mine, mine, mine! Do you hear? Mine forever! Ha ha ha ha ha!

3 Match the speech bubbles (1–8) to the crimes (a–h).

1 *Well, I knew they were away on holiday, so I just broke a window, went in and took what I could carry.* ......

2 *We smashed up an old car. Why? I don't know. It just felt good at the time.* ......

3 *Yeah, his wallet was falling out of his trousers so I just helped it on its way.* ......

4 *I had the photos of him with her, so I demanded £1 million to keep it a secret.* ......

5 *Have you any idea how easy it is? I could hack into your bank account in seconds if they let me have a computer.* ......

6 *Calling me this makes it sound like it's my job, but I only ever killed one person.* ......

7 *So, I copied and sold stuff on the street. How's that more of a crime than you illegally downloading videos at home?* ......

8 *I'm sure you stole something from a shop once, didn't you? Be honest. ... You didn't? Oh. ... Well, I just made it my hobby.* ......

a murderer
b blackmailer
c shoplifter
d pirate
e cybercriminal
f burglar
g vandal
h pickpocket

ALL ABOUT ME

1 If your mobile phone was stolen, would you like to meet the person who stole it? Why?/Why not?

....

2 What online educational course would you study if you were in prison? Why?

....

3 If somebody you knew sprayed graffiti on a wall, would you tell the police? Why?/Why not?

....

1 a Choose the correct option in 1–8.

1 I ***think*** / ***am thought***, therefore
2 To ***be*** / ***being*** or not
3 You must ***to be*** / ***be*** the change
4 You can ***do*** / ***doing*** anything
5 Dance ***is liking*** / ***like***
6 You always ***are missing*** / ***miss*** 100% of the shots
7 The richest man ***being*** / ***is*** not he who has the most,
8 Always ***forgive*** / ***forgave*** your enemies;

a you wish to make in the world.
b but not everything.
c you never take.
d nobody's watching.
e I am.
f but he who needs the least.
g nothing annoys them so much.
h to be – that is the question.

b Now match the sentence halves in Exercise 1a. Write the complete sentences below.

1 ....
2 ....
3 ....
4 ....
5 ....
6 ....
7 ....
8 ....

2 Decide whether the question tag is asking for real information (*I*) or agreement (*A*).

1 I can see that you really like it here, don't you? ....
2 You don't have a clue where we are really, do you? ....
3 There isn't a toilet near here, is there? ....
4 He would say that, wouldn't he? ....
5 You don't know when the next train to Crewe arrives, do you? ....
6 We've been waiting for more than two hours, haven't we? ....
7 You didn't tell her, did you? ....
8 I'm not sure but I think she's Turkish, isn't she? ....

3 These are famous opening lines from books about utopias and dystopias. Choose the correct options to complete the sentences.

1 *Midway upon the journey of our life, I* **found** / **had found** *myself within a dark forest, for the straightforward pathway had* **been** / **being** *lost.*

The Divine Comedy – Dante

2 *As Gregor Samsa awoke from a night of uneasy dreaming, he* **had found** / **found** *himself* **transformed** / **had being transformed** *in his bed into a gigantic insect.*

Metamorphosis – Kafka

3 *It* **was** / **was being** *a bright cold day in April, and the clocks* **were striking** / **had been struck** *thirteen.*

1984 – Orwell

4 *It* **was** / **had** *the best of times, it* **was** / **is being** *the worst of times.*

A Tale of two Cities – Dickens

5 *The boy with fair hair* **lowered** / **had been lowering** *himself down the last few feet of rock and began to* **pick** / **had picked** *his way toward the lagoon.*

Lord of the Flies – Golding

UNIT 8

FRENEMIES

VOCABULARY 1 >>> Talk about relationships

1 Match the people (1–12) to the definitions (a–l).

1 acquaintance ......
2 boyfriend/girlfriend ......
3 classmate ......
4 close friend ......
5 enemy ......
6 friend of a friend ......
7 guest ......
8 neighbour ......
9 old friend ......
10 online friend ......
11 relative ......
12 teammate ......

a a friend that you get on well with, see a lot of and can really trust
b someone you play a sport with who is on the same side as you
c someone who is part of your family
d someone you know but not well enough to call a friend
e someone you don't really know – but your friend knows them well
f someone you probably haven't met in person that you chat with a lot on the internet
g someone you go on dates to the cinema with
h someone you go to school with and who has the same teacher as you
i someone you dislike a lot or someone who really doesn't like you
j someone visiting or staying at your home for a few days
k someone who lives near you, eg in the same street or in the next house
l someone you've known for a long time, eg since your school days (and you're now 50)

2 Complete the sentences with a word or phrase from Exercise 1 and a phrasal verb from the box.

asked ... out fell out ~~going out~~ got on got together let down put up with

1 Edward and Millie are *going out*. They are *boyfriend* and *girlfriend*.
2 Tom and Hannah were ......s. They did everything together but they ...... a few weeks ago.
3 They have never .... In fact, there is real hatred there – she is basically his number one ......
4 I wouldn't call him a friend; more a(n) .... I like him but I find it difficult to ...... his sense of humour, and we don't really know each other that well.
5 He ...... his ......s by getting a red card. They could have won.
6 I have ......s – my aunt and uncle – who ...... on a TV show.
7 She's a(n) .... We've never met but we get on well. I ...... her ...... but she said she just wants to stay friends.

3 Complete the rules about phrasal verbs with the words in the box.

after between have an object

- When phrasal verbs are transitive ((1) ......), the object can go in different positions.
  – With *ask somebody out* and *let somebody down*, the object goes (2) ...... the verb and adverb.
  – With *put up with somebody* and *get over somebody*, the object comes (3) ...... the preposition.

4 Replace the words and phrases in *italics* with the correct form of the phrasal verbs in the box.

break up with fall out with get on (well) with get over go out with let down make up with ~~put up with~~

1 I can't *tolerate* her anymore. She's so annoying! *put up with*
2 I've started *dating* Kyle. He's really lovely. ......
3 I *have a good relationship with* Mike. We laugh at the same things. ......
4 I *stopped being friendly with* Luke after we had that big argument. ......
5 She has *separated from* Paul – I feel so sad for both of them. ......
6 You always *make* me *disappointed*. I can't rely on you. ......
7 We apologised to each other. I'*m friends* with Julie *again*. ......
8 I've *forgotten* Mia. I feel happy again – my new girlfriend is so kind and sweet. ......

READING

Recognise facts and opinions

1 Complete the tips with the words in the box.

REMEMBER HOW TO ...

recognise facts and opinions

checked feelings statistics text type

- Look at the (1) ________ : Decide if it usually has facts, opinions or both.
- Facts can be (2) ________ . Look for (3) ________ , sources or phrases like *According to, Research shows.*
- Opinions are based on (4) ________ and experiences. Look for phrases like *I think, In my opinion/experience.*

2 Number the sentences in the paragraph in the correct order.

____ a After birth, the human brain grows rapidly*, more than doubling* to reach 60% of its adult size by the time a child is one.

____ b But the grey matter, or thinking part of the brain, continues to develop until the age of 11 in girls and 12 in boys.

____ c By the age of six, the brain is already 95% of its adult size.

____ d Even then, the brain never stops changing, for better or worse.

____ e From birth through to adulthood our brains go on an amazing journey, and scientists are discovering much more about how and when the brain develops.

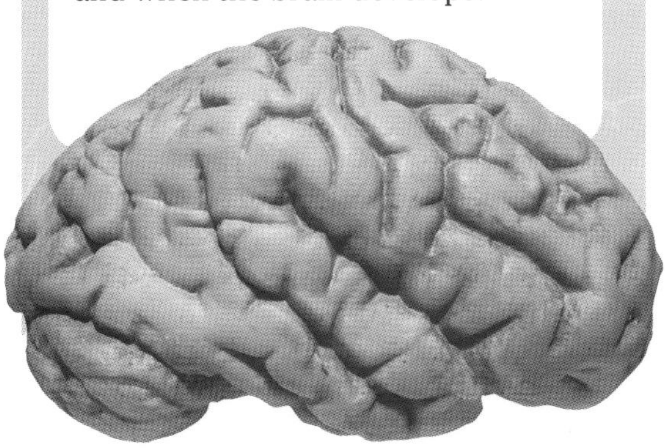

Glossary
*__rapidly__ = quickly
*__doubling__ = increasing in size by twice the amount.

3 Which of the sentences (a–e) in Exercise 2 contain facts (*F*) and which contain both facts and opinions (*F/O*)?

a *F* b ____ c ____ d ____ e ____

4 Now read the rest of the article and decide whether the highlighted sections are fact (*F*) or opinion (*O*).

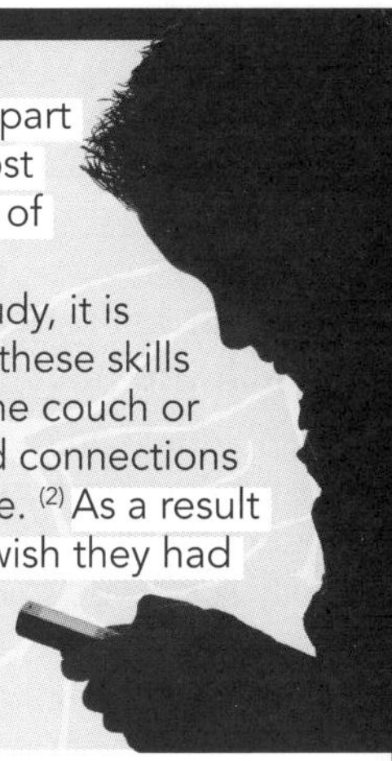

(1) The next stage, when the thinking part is still developing, is perhaps the most interesting, because there is a sense of 'use it or lose it'. *O*
If a teen is doing music, sports or study, it is the cells and connections related to these skills that will do well. If they're lying on the couch or playing video games, these cells and connections are the ones that are going to survive. (2) As a result some people, later in life, may well wish they had worked on important life skills from a younger age. ____

One part of the brain that develops much later is the front part. (3) It's involved in things like planning and decision making. ____ So it's perhaps no wonder that many teens have arguments with their parents about focusing on tasks or finishing things. Planning what to do, where and when is important to an adult, but teenagers are perhaps less concerned about this.

So when exactly do we become good decision-makers? (4) Recent research into how the brain develops suggests that people can make big life decisions better in their late 20s. ____ 'Until very recently, we had to make some pretty important life decisions about education and career paths, who to marry and whether to go into the army at a time when parts of our brains were not optimal* yet,' says neuroscientist Jay Giedd. (5) 'Delaying those decisions makes sense biologically*,' he says. ____

Glossary
*__optimal__ = the best / at the best level
*__biologically__ = in relation to the human body and its natural processes

5 Read the text again and think about these questions.

1 What have you been doing as a teenager? How will this affect the skills you develop? Do you think you will regret not practising some skills more?
2 Do you have arguments with your parents about your planning and organising? If so, what was your last argument about?

GO BEYOND

Research when the brain's power is at its best and also when it gets worse. Find out about the following topics at different stages of our life and make notes in your notebook.

- brain speed
- memory
- knowledge

GRAMMAR 1 Wishes and regrets: *I wish* and *If only*

Talk about wishes and regrets

1 Complete the grammar table with the words in the box.

past (x2) present unhappiness

Wishes and regrets: *I wish* and *If only*
Use: To express (1) .... with a situation in the (2) .... or the past.
Form: present *I wish / If only* + (3) .... simple
Form: past *I wish / If only* + (4) .... perfect

2 Look at the sentences and decide which are present regrets (*Pr*) and which are past regrets (*Pa*).

1 I wish I could go out. Pr
2 I wish I had more money. ......
3 If only I'd had more time to prepare for my interview. ......
4 If only I'd stayed in bed longer. ......
5 If only I were taller, I could play more sports. ......
6 I wish I lived in a big city. ......
7 I wish the car hadn't broken down. ......
8 If only I wasn't so tired. ......
9 I wish you hadn't lost my camera. ......
10 If only you'd been more careful that night. ......

3 › Complete the sentences with the verbs in the box.

'd done 'd eaten 'd gone out 'd had 'd listened 'd never started 'd studied hadn't eaten

1 I wish I .... training for the marathon. Once you start running, you can't stop!
2 I wish I .... to my parents.
3 I wish I .... a brother or sister to chat to when I was growing up.
4 I wish I .... harder at school. Then I'd have a better job.
5 I wish I .... so much. I feel sick.
6 I wish I .... breakfast because it's not even lunchtime and I need something to eat.
7 I wish I .... my homework.
8 I wish I .... last night. The party sounded like fun.

4 › Match each speech bubble to a regret (1–8) in Exercise 3.

a 8 *I was so bored at home watching TV.*

b ...... *It was boring being an only child.*

c ...... *I feel terrible now – really unwell.*

d ...... *I'm really hungry now.*

e ...... *The teacher isn't going to be happy.*

f ...... *I can't give it up now – I want to get faster!*

g ...... *I could've got a better job.*

h ...... *They were right about this job.*

5 ›› Use *wish* and a past tense form to write about Cathy's feelings.

1 (She can't concentrate.)
I wish I could concentrate.
2 (She gets angry quickly.)
________ so angry.
3 (She is so tired.) ________
4 (Her friend isn't speaking to her.)
________ my friend
________.
5 (Her friends aren't honest.)
____
6 (Her essay isn't going well.)
________ better.
7 (She isn't feeling well.) ________
better.
8 (She has a French speaking test.)
________ for my French exam.

6 ›› Complete the sentences with the correct past perfect form of the phrasal verbs in the box.

~~break up~~ fall out get on get over get together make up

1 I really miss him. I wish we *hadn't broken up* and we were still together.
2 I met my first boyfriend at university. I hated him in the end. I wish I ________ with him in the first place.
3 I argued a lot with my parents when I was young. I wish I ________ better with them.
4 We had an argument and never spoke again. I wish we ________ and we were still friends.
5 I wanted to be friends again. I wish we ________ but we never spoke again.
6 I can't forget him. I wish I ________ him but I'm always thinking about him.

7 ››› Complete the conversation with the correct form of the verbs in brackets.

Paula: I feel really bad today.
Lucia: Why?
Paula: I shouted at Salvatore. I really wish I (1) *hadn't shouted* (shout) at him.
Lucia: What did you say to him?
Paula: I said 'I wish you (2) ________ (be) so lazy. My life would be so much better if I (3) ________ (meet) you.'
Lucia: Really! You wish you (4) ________ (meet) him?
Paula: Of course not! I'm so glad I met him, but he drives me crazy. If only he (5) ________ (put) more effort into our relationship. The worst thing is that it was in front of his friends.
Lucia: You mean, you shouted at him in front of his friends?
Paula: Yep …
Lucia: Oh, no!
Paula: I know. Do you think he'll break up with me?
Lucia: He might. If only his friends (6) ________ (be) there, it might have been OK.
Paula: I wish I (7) ________ (stay) calm. If only I (8) ________ (phone) him now.
Lucia: Why can't you?
Paula: I was so angry that I deleted his number …

LISTENING

Understand hesitation

1 Complete the tips with the words and phrases in the box.

REMEMBER HOW TO …

understand hesitation

hold on I mean thinking What's the word? words

- Listen for sounds like *um, er, ah, eh* and words like *well, you know,* (1) ________ , *like, kind of,* (2) ________ and *actually*. The speaker is (3) ________ what to say.
- Listen for phrases like *What do you call it?* (4) ________ , *How do you say it?* The speaker is trying to find the right (5) ________ .
- Listen carefully to what the speaker says next.

2 ▶32 Listen to the conversation. What's happening? Choose the correct option.

a Someone is being asked out.
b Someone is breaking up with their partner.
c Someone has been let down by their friend.

3 ▶32 Listen again and complete the sentences.

No, (1) ________ …
(2) ________ I think we need to take a break from each other.

(3) ________ , I still like you and everything but, (4) ________ , we do spend a lot of time together and that's, (5) ________ … um … a bit too much sometimes.

(6) ________ , I'm sorry. It's not you – it's (7) ________ me.

4 a Complete the conversation below with the words and expressions in the box. (There are no right answers – you decide.)

I mean like (x2) um well you know

Luke: Hi Mike, I've … (1) ________ … got something to, (2) ________ , tell you.
Mike: What's that then?
Luke: You know … um … your ex-girlfriend – eh … Carla, (3) ________ .
Mike: Yes. What about her?
Luke: Well, you've got over her (4) ________ , haven't you?
Mike: Of course, why?
Luke: Actually, (5) ________ , I've … um … started going out with her.
Mike: What?! When did that happen?
Luke: We, (6) ________ , got together … um … a few … weeks ago.
Mike: But I only broke up with her five weeks ago.
Luke: I started … like … seeing her … um … about four weeks ago.

b ▶33 Listen and compare the words or phrases you hear to the ones you used.

c Now write the exact words and phrases you heard for gaps 1–6 above.

1 ________ 3 ________ 5 ________
2 ________ 4 ________ 6 ________

5 Imagine telling one of your parents you failed a test. Write a conversation between you and them. Use at least eight filler words (eg *I mean*) and/or hesitation phrases (eg *um*).

VOCABULARY 2

Reporting verbs

1 Match the verbs to the definitions.

1 accuse ......
2 blame ......
3 forgive ......
4 offer ......
5 refuse ......
6 threaten ......
7 warn ......
8 persuade ......
9 advise ......
10 remind ......

a to decide that you will not be angry with someone who has angered, upset or harmed you
b to tell someone that you might or you will cause them harm, especially in order to make them do something
c to get someone to agree to do something by giving them reasons why they should
d to say that someone has done something wrong or committed a crime
e to give your opinion to someone about the best thing to do in a particular situation
f to tell someone again about something that they may have forgotten or information they used to know
g to say or think that someone or something is responsible for an accident, problem or bad situation
h to make someone aware of a possible problem or danger so that they will not be hurt
i to let someone know that you will give them something (eg help) if they want it
j to say you will not do something that someone has asked you to do

2 Complete the sentences with the past simple form of the verb in brackets and a preposition.

1 He *accused* (accuse) her *of* being lazy.
2 Sonia .... (blame) Maria .... telling everyone.
3 Jessica .... (forgive) Mike .... breaking up with her.
4 Paul .... (offer) .... play in their team.
5 Jane .... (refuse) .... see him.
6 Katie .... (threaten) .... tell everyone.
7 Harry .... (warn) him .... (not) open her mail.
8 She finally .... (persuade) Frank .... calm down.
9 They .... (advise) Sally .... make up with Simon.
10 David .... (remind) John not .... let them down again.

WORDS & BEYOND

3 Complete Nikki's letter and Zoe's reply with the words in the box.

contact control date desperately get down in the dumps give (somebody) some space overheard upset

Dear Zoe,
I went on a (1) .... with a boy the other day and I (2) .... want to see him again. I've tried to (3) .... him but he hasn't replied. I'm worried now because I (4) .... two girls saying I'm desperate and should leave him alone. What should I do?
Nikki

Dear Nikki,
Try not to be (5) .... about what you heard the other girls say. Gossip will always happen. There might be a reason why this boy hasn't contacted you but you can't (6) .... what he does. Try to (7) .... him .... and perhaps he will contact you. Anyway, don't (8) .... – there will be other people.
Best wishes,
Zoe

4 Complete the school policy document with the words in the box.

bully care caring depression face-to-face feedback go without policy praise role models

Highdown School Bullying (1) ....

We take great (2) .... in dealing with bullying in our school. Should we receive any (3) .... indicating that someone is a (4) ...., we will investigate the claims fully. Both the accused bully and the victim will meet (5) .... individually with the headteacher. Bullying can cause serious problems like (6) .... and will not (7) .... punishment. We wish to establish a (8) .... environment for all our students.
As part of this, we (9) .... people who are (10) .... in our campaign against bullying and will recognise their good work in reports to parents.

GRAMMAR 2 Reported speech review

»» Report what other people say

1 Complete the grammar table with the words and phrases in the box.

commands if/whether requests
subject what/who, etc

Reported speech
Use: To report what people said in direct speech.
Form: statements *told me / said (that)* + (1) .... + verb Use the past form of verbs and change pronouns, etc. *'Luke told me.'* → *He said that Luke had told him.*
Form: *wh-* questions *asked me* + (2) .... + subject + verb *'What are you talking about?'* → *I asked him what he was talking about.*
Form: *yes/no* questions *asked me* + (3) .... + subject + verb *'Is it true?'* → *He asked me whether it was true.*
Form: (4) .... *asked me* + *(not) to* + infinitive *'Please explain.'* → *I asked him to explain.*
Form: (5) .... *told me* + *(not) to* + infinitive *'Tell me what's so funny.'* → *He told me to tell him what was so funny.*

2 Match each example of direct speech (1–10) to the correct form (a–e).

1 'Tell her to keep it a secret.' ......
2 'Please leave.' ......
3 'What will happen to bullies?' ......
4 'Is she right?' ......
5 'Did she tell the truth?' ......
6 'Tell her to be quiet.' ......
7 'Please don't say anything.' ......
8 'What did she say?' ......
9 'Lisa wants to meet you.' ......
10 'John answered the phone.' ......

a statement
b *Wh-* questions
c *yes/no* questions
d requests
e commands

3 » Write the sentences in Exercise 2 in reported speech.

1 I *told her* to *keep it a secret*.
2 I .... her ....
3 I ....
4 I ....
5 I ....
6 He .... me ....
7 She .... them ....
8 I .... him ....
9 She .... Lisa .... me.
10 He .... John ....

4 »» Find and correct the mistakes in the sentences.

1 The doctor told him take more exercise.
....
2 He wanted to know if the special price that night includes the internet.
....
3 She asked us whether that we had eaten lunch.
....
4 Colin said me he wanted to come with us.
....
5 Rachel said she did liked her new phone.
....
6 Helen asked us for not to gossip.
....
7 They told they were from the police.
....
8 He ask me if he was right.
....

Express regret and forgiveness

1 Look at the phrases in *italics* in the conversation. Decide which are expressions of regret (*R*) and which are expressions of forgiveness (*F*).

Theo: Hi Shadia. (1) *I apologise for* R calling so late in the evening.
Shadia: (2) *That's OK. Don't worry.* ___ What's up?
Theo: (3) *I feel bad about* ___ our presentation today. (4) *I really regret letting you down.* ___
Shadia: (5) *You couldn't help it.* ___ You were nervous anyway, and then when Mo and Ahmed sat there talking all the time it was very hard to concentrate.
Theo: I know. I still feel bad. (6) *It won't happen again – I promise.* ___
Shadia: (7) *Seriously, don't worry.* ___ (8) *It wasn't your fault.* ___
Theo: So you'd work with me again?
Shadia: Of course!

2 (34) Listen and practise reading the conversation out loud. Pay attention to intonation.

3 (35) Listen to three conversations. Match each conversation to the thing one of the speakers regrets.

Conversation 1 ___ a letting someone down
Conversation 2 ___ b getting angry
Conversation 3 ___ c upsetting someone

4 Complete the *Phrasebook* with the words in the box.

awful matter shouted told upset upsetting

5 a (35) Listen again and check.

b (36) Listen to the phrases and repeat, paying attention to intonation.

6 Look at the situations below. Choose one and write a short conversation expressing regret and forgiveness.

a forgetting someone's birthday
b being late
c missing a deadline
d posting an embarrassing photo online

7 Read your conversation out loud and focus on your use of intonation. Record yourself if you can.

PHRASEBOOK

Express regret

I wish I'd / I hadn't (1) ___ you … (clue: 'said it to you')

I'm sorry if I (2) ___ you.

I feel (3) ___ / really bad about it …

I should/shouldn't have (4) ___ …

I'm really sorry for (5) ___ you.

Express forgiveness

Don't worry about it.

It doesn't (6) ___ . / That's all right.

WRITING

Add detail to a description

1 Complete the tips with the words and phrases in the box.

REMEMBER HOW TO ...

add detail to a description

as fast as lightning creep isn't your cup of tea it looked as if a toddler had built it run a mile from strict walk wonderful

- Use adjectives (eg *cheerful, generous*, (1) ______, (2) ______). ☐
- Use descriptive verbs (*whisper* instead of *say*, *giggle* instead of *laugh*, (3) ______ instead of (4) ______). ☐
- Use idioms (eg (5) ______, (6) ______). ☐
- Use similes (eg *as busy as a bee*, (7) ______, (8) ______). ☐

2 Read the magazine extract. What does the magazine want readers to post articles about on its website? Choose the correct option, a, b or c.

a What inspires them in life.
b A person who inspires them in life.
c The time when they were most inspired in their life.

To be a role model in someone's life is (1)easier said than done. Think about your role models growing up. We want to know about someone who inspired you. They may have been there for you – (2)a class act or good role model – throughout your life, or they may have been (3)a breath of fresh air in a dull situation. Was there someone (4)as fit as a fiddle that started you off in a sport or helped to lead you down the path to a healthier lifestyle? Did you meet someone (5)as brave as a lion who made you forget or face your fears? Or did you meet someone (6)as bright as a button, who inspired you to use your mind and get the most out of your schooling? We want to know. Post your article on our website now. The best article (chosen by our editors) will win a prize.

3 Look at the underlined expressions in Exercise 2. Decide which ones are similes (*S*) and which are idioms (*I*).

1 easier said than done ___
2 a class act ___
3 a breath of fresh air ___
4 as fit as a fiddle ___
5 as brave as a lion ___
6 as bright as a button ___

4 Use the idioms and similes underlined in Exercise 2 to complete these reader comments.

Being my teacher was (1) ______ as I wasn't a very good student. But Mr Holiday made me believe in myself and was always *cheerful*.

My football coach was (2) ______ when he joined us. Training had been so boring before. He *bounced around* with energy and was really *positive* – lots of fresh new ideas. He made us feel like (3) ______ even though we were *rubbish* – I mean, we were really, really bad.

My dad was seriously ill but he was (4) ______ and *fought back*. Afterwards he *grabbed* every opportunity in life. He started running marathons and became (5) ______ .

My sister is (6) ______ – probably the most intelligent person I know. She never acts like she's better than anyone and she gets on with everyone.

5 Look at the words and phrases in *italics* in the comments in Exercise 4. Match each one to its meaning below.

1 full of confidence and hope *positive*
2 recovered ______
3 took ______
4 happy ______
5 a very low standard or quality ______
6 moved with energy and enthusiasm ______

WRITING PLAN

6 a You're going to write an article about a role model. Think about a person who has inspired you in your life. Use the *Writing plan* to help you prepare.

WRITING PLAN

Make notes for your article.

Paragraph 1: Say who they are. ☐

Paragraph 2: Say what their positive qualities are. ☐

Paragraph 3: Say what they did/do that inspires you. ☐

Paragraph 4: Say how they behave that inspires you. ☐

b Read the tips in the *Remember how to* box again and think of descriptive language to include in your answer.

WRITE AND CHECK

7 Write your article. Then tick (✓) the stages in the *Writing plan*.

Give and accept feedback

1 Look at the statements. Decide if the advice relates to *giving feedback* (G) or *accepting feedback* (A).

1 Others might be right and you might be wrong. *A*
2 Show care and consideration for others when you comment on their performance. ____
3 Be open to change and prepared to make changes in how you do things. ____
4 Be honest with yourself and know when to listen. ____
5 Concentrate on the behaviour not the person. ____
6 Be realistic in your comments by focusing on what can change. ____

2 Read about Ana's situation. Do you think she's good at accepting feedback? Underline the information that helps you decide. ____

Ana had to work on a group project with other students from her class. Afterwards the teacher asked each group member to provide comments on the other members' work. Several members of Ana's group said that she needed to spend more time perfecting her work and that it was a bit hurried. Ana didn't really think this was true. She believes that spending a long time doing things is too big a priority* for some people. She's sure she can do things just as well in half the amount of time as most people. She has always done well working like this and can't see any reason to change.

Glossary
***priority** = being very important

3 What advice would you give Ana?

____
____
____
____

1 Read and complete the sentences with money-related words. Use present tense verb forms.

1 I d.................. £20 to charity every month.
2 We need to r.................. money to repair the roof of the youth centre.
3 How much shall I w.................. from the cash machine?
4 I need to p.................. you b.................. the money I borrowed.
5 I'm going to i.................. my uncle's house when he dies.
6 Here's the £10 I o.................. you. Thanks very much.
7 My i.................. is not great, but I don't work much overtime.
8 When a company's successful it makes a p.................., but when it's unsuccessful it makes a l.................. .

2 Find the words from Exercise 1 in the word search.

P	A	Y	B	A	C	K	W	R	L
T	I	F	O	R	P	I	A	Y	O
D	Q	M	U	T	T	I	N	A	S
C	G	Y	X	H	S	X	O	E	S
F	J	F	D	E	F	I	R	W	B
W	B	R	T	I	R	E	H	N	I
R	A	I	N	C	O	M	E	U	C
W	I	K	G	B	L	E	T	O	L
A	D	O	N	A	T	E	D	W	Y
N	K	J	K	L	Z	Q	J	E	W

3 Match what the people say (1–8) to the words and phrases (a–h).

1 'He was given a £200 fine.' ......
2 'There's very little crime where I live.' ......
3 'What did he say when he saw the damage to his car?' ......
4 'There are a lot of problems in that area.' ......
5 'I can't find my phone, wallet or keys.' ......
6 'The police have closed off the area.' ......
7 'He is one of the most wanted people in the world.' ......
8 'They made an illegal payment to get the contract.' ......

a crime scene
b punishment
c mafia boss
d corruption
e neighbourhood
f valuables
g trouble spot
h owner

4 a Decide which adjectives form a word that has the opposite meaning when you change the ending to *-ful*/*-less*. Tick (✓) them.

1 careful ☐
2 grateful ☐
3 endless ☐
4 motionless ☐
5 forgetful ☐
6 peaceful ☐
7 helpless ☐
8 pointless ☐
9 hopeless ☐
10 stressful ☐

b Complete the sentences with the adjectives (1–10) from Exercise 4a.

1 It's .... asking me – I don't know the answer either.
2 You're so .... – lucky I reminded you about that maths exam.
3 I'm really .... – thanks for all your help.
4 It's so .... here – there's no-one around.
5 I don't find exams .... – I'm confident in my ability.
6 We found a poor .... puppy crying for its mother at the bottom of our garden.
7 You should be more .... – you could hurt yourself doing that.
8 I was so scared I just stood there .... for several minutes.
9 You ask a(n) .... number of questions – enough already!
10 It's a(n) .... situation – I don't know what to do.

ALL ABOUT ME

1 What things in life make you grateful?

....

2 When was the last time you were careless?

....

3 What things in life do you find stressful?

....

1 Rewrite the sentences using *if* + *will/can*.

1 You might fail the speaking test. You can take it again.
If you *fail the speaking test, you can take it again.*
2 We need to catch the bus. We need to hurry.
If we ______.
3 Do you need a ticket? I can get you one.
If you ______.
4 Apologise or I won't speak to you again.
If you don't ______.
5 You're not allowed to gossip. They might kick you out of school.
If you ______, you ______.
6 Is he entering the race? He'll probably win.
If he ______.
7 I might need time off work. I'm sure my boss will give it to me.
If I ______.

2 Choose the correct options below to complete the conversation.

Frank: Sorry I can't come to your party. If I (1) ___ to work, I (2) ___.
Lisa: Don't worry. If you (3) ___, you (4) ___ dinner for me some time instead.
Frank: OK, sure. Or, if you (5) ___, I can take you out for dinner.
Lisa: That sounds great. Some of the others can't come to Manchester now either. Would you mind if I (6) ___ them out for dinner with us instead?
Frank: That's fine. Who else can't come?
Lisa: Ghanem, Raul, Steve, Tina and Susie.
Frank: Raul, really? If you invite him, I (7) ___. I'm not speaking to him since he let me down.
Lisa: Oh, come on! If he (8) ___ you sooner, you would've forgiven him.

	a	b	c	d
1	a don't have	b hadn't	c didn't have	d haven't had
2	a come	b would come	c will come	d came
3	a can't come	b haven't come	c hadn't come	d can come
4	a will cook	b can cook	c cook	d cooked
5	a wanted	b will	c can	d want
6	a invited	b had invited	c have invited	d shall invite
7	a not come	b won't come	c can't come	d hadn't come
8	a phoned	b will phone	c won't phone	d had phoned

3 Correct the mistakes in *italics* in the sentences.

1 Rita might have gone to the gig if she *knew* her favourite singer was performing. ______
2 If you hadn't woken me up last night, I *wouldn't been* so tired this morning. ______
3 If you *will go*, I will come as well. ______
4 If you *would wait*, I could come with you. ______
5 If she doesn't arrive soon, I *go* home – I'm tired of waiting for her here. ______
6 If I*'d eat* cake every day, I'd get fat. ______

4 Match the sentences and join them with *if*. What type of conditional is each one? Write your answers below.

1 I left too late.
2 You don't take an umbrella.
3 You give me directions.
4 I drank coffee late.
5 I didn't like the food.
6 I nearly dropped the computer.

a You might get wet.
b I wouldn't eat it.
c I missed the bus.
d It would have been a disaster.
e I wouldn't be able to sleep.
f I'll try to follow them.

1 *[1c] If I hadn't left too late, I wouldn't have missed the bus. (3rd conditional)*
2 ______
3 ______
4 ______
5 ______
6 ______

UNIT 9

LOOK AFTER YOURSELF

VOCABULARY 1 >>> Talk about street food and how it's made

1 Read the clues and complete the words. Then check your answers by finding them in the word search.

1 c ________ (a thin, flat, usually round cake made from flour, milk and eggs)
2 p ________ (spaghetti and lasagne are types of this food)
3 p ________ (a roundish vegetable that grows underground)
4 p ________ (a popular Italian food – not pasta!)
5 p ____ (a pastry dish filled with meat, vegetables or fruit)
6 c ________ (fried potatoes)
7 b ________ (small seeds of climbing vegetables)
8 t ______ (a type of fish)
9 s ________ (a Japanese food)
10 e ____ (what came first – the chicken or this?)

P	S	P	Y	L	D	M	G	E	P
G	O	E	D	O	A	E	V	N	I
U	A	T	G	G	E	T	P	K	Z
B	N	J	A	T	L	O	S	V	Z
E	U	U	M	T	S	S	L	A	A
A	T	P	N	U	O	P	F	C	P
N	T	O	S	I	D	I	G	R	K
S	S	H	E	F	L	H	Z	E	F
O	I	F	I	I	F	C	K	P	H
O	L	G	P	K	L	I	K	E	B

2 Match the words (1–8) to the pictures (a–h).

1 baked ____
2 boiled ____
3 steamed ____
4 grilled ____
5 filled ____
6 wrapped ____
7 spread ____
8 fried ____

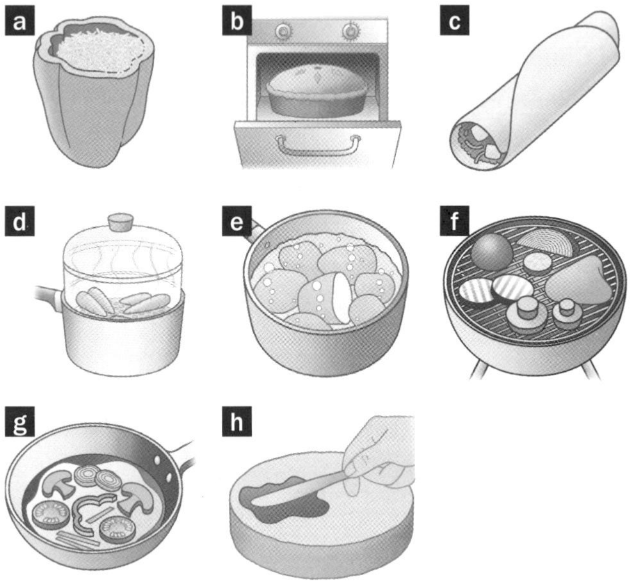

3 Complete the paragraph with the words in the box.

bake boil fry grill steam

Now, as far as I'm concerned, the healthiest way to cook vegetables is to (1) ________ them over a pot of boiling water. If you (2) ________ them actually in the water, they lose a lot of their nutritional value. We've all been told that to (3) ________ food in oil is not so good for you, but if you use a wok*, and cut up everything into small pieces, you can cook it quickly and it's healthy. As far as using an oven is concerned, food that you (4) ________ or roast takes time. But, if you have one in your garden, there's the barbecue option. What smells better than meat or vegetables that you (5) ________ over a charcoal fire!

Glossary
*__wok__ = a metal pan shaped like a large bowl, used for cooking Chinese food

4 Choose the best option to complete the sentences.

1 *I like my vegetables* **crunchy / spread**, *don't you? They keep their goodness that way.*

2 *I like to make my own pizza so I can put whatever* **filling / topping** *I want on it.*

3 *For me, the hotter, the better – I just love* **spicy / bitter** *Indian food.*

4 *Have you checked the date on this milk? It tastes* **savoury / sour** *to me.*

5 *What's your favourite sandwich* **filling / wrapping**?

6 *Wow, this coffee is so* **sweet / bitter** *– pass the sugar, please.*

READING

Recognise reasons and results

1 Complete the tips with the words in the box.

REMEMBER HOW TO ...

recognise reasons and results

as as a consequence as a result because (of) due to since so therefore

- Look for linking expressions:
  1 For results: ________ ________ ________ ________
  2 For reasons: ________ ________ ________ ________
- Look for verbs that introduce results like *cause*, *change*, *produce*, *make* and *result in*.

2 Choose the correct option to complete the sentences.

1 I became overweight ***because*** / ***so*** I ate too much.
2 I ate too much ***because*** / ***so*** I became overweight.
3 I'm full. ***As*** / ***Therefore*** , I can't finish this meal.
4 I'm late for work. ***As a consequence*** / ***Due to*** , I won't have breakfast.
5 ***Since*** / ***So*** I won't have breakfast, I'll go for a nice lunch.

3 Read the text and choose the best title.

a Why children are obese
b What governments do wrong
c How to provide better school facilities

4 What type of text is this? Choose the most likely answer.

a an information leaflet
b an advertisement
c a newspaper opinion article

5 Read the first three paragraphs again and complete these sentences. Choose from the verbs and linking expressions in bold.

1 Obesity is sometimes *caused* by a bad diet, which can ________ diseases.
2 ________ government cutbacks, there is a lack of facilities.
3 ________ the state doesn't provide these facilities, others can ________ things.

6 a Read paragraphs 4 and 5. Find seven linking expressions and one verb that show reasons or results. Write them in the order they appear in the text.

	Reason	Result
1		
2		
3		
4		
5		
6		
7		
8		

b Tick (✓) whether each shows a reason or a result.

7 Look at the underlined words in the text. Write each underlined word next to its meaning (1–4).

1 very many ________
2 frightening/worrying ________
3 big/important ________
4 a place that serves food in a school, office, etc ________

GO BEYOND

Research sponsorship in schools and make notes in your notebook about where it happens and how it works.

[1]It is vitally important that our young people today have the opportunity to take part in sport and eat healthily. Although there are genetic factors beyond our control, the alarming rise in child obesity levels is mostly **caused** by a lack of exercise and a bad diet. And we know, unfortunately, that obesity can **result in** serious diseases and issues of mental health (especially when children are bullied by cruel classmates for being different).

[2]**As a consequence of** government cutbacks over the years, many schools no longer have open green areas for sports, covered gymnasiums or canteens offering a cooked lunch. **Since** the state can't or won't provide these facilities, the private sector can step in to help to **change** what has become a national problem.

[3]I have looked into what happens in other countries and have found that major supermarket chains, sports-goods manufacturers as well as smaller local shops and businesses are keen to sponsor* food and sports facilities in schools. They have **made** a definite difference and enabled countless schools to offer what they couldn't before **because of** a lack of money.

[4]Sponsorship works abroad, so it could happen here. Why doesn't it? I think it's due to two things. Firstly, fears that fast food companies could become sponsors and, as a result, force our children to eat unhealthy meals. Well, we don't need to worry about that as we would choose the sponsors and ensure good quality. Secondly, it's because we are uncomfortable with the idea of commercialisation and private involvement in state education. Yes, in an ideal world the government would provide every school with the best facilities, but, as this doesn't happen, we have to look for alternatives.

[5]Finding the right ones will help us produce a healthier, fitter new generation. Therefore, let's at least consider the role the private sector could play in achieving this.

Glossary

*sponsor = a person, company or organisation that provides support by giving money or help

GRAMMAR 1 Modal passives

Use the passive form of modal verbs

1 Complete the grammar table with the phrases in the box.

have been modal verb more important past participle

Modal passives
Use: With a (1) .... when the action is (2) .... than the person that does the action.
Form: present and future modal verb + *be* + (3) ....
Form: past modal verb + (4) .... + past participle

2 Tick (✓) the sentences that use modal passives and put a cross (✗) beside the ones that don't.

1 They should label all food properly. ☐
2 The waiter should not have served us our food undercooked. ☐
3 This restaurant should have been closed down years ago. ☐
4 I booked us a table at *Haugh's* for 8pm. ☐
5 A table for the wrong number of people must have been booked. ☐

3 › Match the sentence halves.

1 Money should be given to schools ......
2 Vegetarian options must be offered ......
3 Nothing will be done about the canteen ......
4 Cookery might have been useful, ...
5 The salt must have been confused with the sugar, ...
6 You would have been told already ......

a unless we organise a petition*.
b so they can provide free lunch for students.
c but we didn't have that subject at school.
d which is why this tea tastes awful.
e if I'd had any news about our restaurant review.
f on all flights from now on.

Glossary
***petition** = a document signed by a large number of people asking for some action to be taken

4 › Choose the correct option to complete the sentences.

1 Heart problems can be ***caused*** / ***causing*** by eating too much salt.
2 Junk food stalls shouldn't ***allow*** / ***be allowed*** to sell to children.
3 Your arteries ***could*** / ***should*** be blocked by bad fat – you may need an operation.
4 Action must ***be*** / ***have been*** taken soon. Otherwise, the problem will get out of control.
5 Chemicals ***could*** / ***can*** have been added to the animals' diet. That would explain the mystery illness.
6 That food last night ***must*** / ***can't*** have been well cooked – I feel terrible.
7 We ***must*** / ***should*** have been informed, but we weren't.
8 The food would ***have*** / ***had*** been brought faster if there were more waiters.

5 » Complete the conversation with the phrases in the box.

can be found	could have been made up
couldn't have been created	must be added
must be sent	should be cooked
won't be spoken to	won't have been heard of

Jamie: Your stupid cookery book is full of ingredients I don't know and that (1) .... by any normal person.

Pierre: I (2) .... like that! Especially by someone whose recipes (3) .... by a ten-year-old child! My superb dishes (4) .... without years of hard work searching for the best ingredients worldwide.

Jamie: Come on! The best stuff (5) .... in your local street market.

Pierre: You may think so, but, to find out the way food (6) .... , I have to see it being made by the local people in their own environment. That's why I (7) .... all around the world for my TV series. Then what (8) .... is that special 'Pierre' touch.

Jamie: No. Just get some local stuff, cut it up, mix in a few herbs or spices and heat it up. Then you've got food. What could be simpler?

6 » Rearrange the words to make sentences.

1 carried / must / dogs / be / .

....

2 here / must / bought / be / food / here / consumed / .

....

3 ten minutes / vegetables / not / be / should / more than / boiled / for / .

....

4 applicants / be / will / notified / by / successful / email / .

....

5 delayed / may / trains / snow / the track / on / be / due to / .

....

6 away / here / taken / food / be / can / eaten / or / .

....

7 »» Complete the conversation with a modal verb in the positive or negative form and *be* or *have been*.

Eva: You know, honey, last night (1) *could have been* better planned, don't you think?

Phil: Well, for a start, sweetheart, we definitely (2) .... left outside the bar in the rain with no taxis around at such an hour. Then when we got to the restaurant, we (3) .... brought something to drink while we were waiting for the food. If they'd been told when to expect us, we (4) .... made to wait for a table, I'm sure. Also, the band (5) .... allowed to play so loudly. I couldn't hear myself think!

Eva: It's probably better that way, isn't it, sugar? But I thought you (6) .... reminded of home when you heard a nice bit of bouzouki music.

Phil: Can't stand the stuff. Why do you think I left? Of course, if I had my way, my dearest, such a horrible noise (7) .... allowed in public places ... ever.

Eva: Perhaps it (8) .... banned. I'll see what I can do. I am the Queen, after all!

LISTENING

Understand the speaker's attitude

1 Complete the tips with the words in the box.

REMEMBER HOW TO ...

understand the speaker's attitude

express interesting listener opposite
polite questions respect topic

- Speakers with a positive attitude towards the (1) ______ are (2) ______, don't (3) ______ negative emotions and (4) ______ turn-taking.
- Speakers with a positive attitude towards the (5) ______ use phrases like *Really?* and *That's* (6) ______, and ask (7) ______.
- Speakers with a negative attitude do the (8) ______.

2 ▶37 Listen to the first conversation and answer the questions.

1 Is the attitude of the man positive (*P*) or negative (*N*)?

______

2 Tick (✓) the two most polite responses. (Use what you heard in the recording to help you.)

a How may I help you? ☐
b What do you want? ☐
c Don't you know that ... ☐
d I'm afraid that ... ☐

3 ▶38 Listen to the second conversation and answer the questions.

1 Is the attitude of the woman positive (*P*) or negative (*N*)? ______
2 Does she express a negative attitude towards the food or David? ______
3 Does the woman respect turn-taking? (*Yes/No*)

______

4 ▶39 Listen to the third conversation and answer the questions.

1 Is the attitude of the woman positive (*P*) or negative (*N*)? ______
2 How many questions does the woman ask?

______

3 Do all the questions show a positive attitude? (*Yes/No*) ______

5 ▶40 Listen to the fourth conversation and answer the questions.

1 Is the attitude of the woman positive (*P*) or negative (*N*)? ______
2 Does the woman respect turn-taking? (*Yes/No*) ______

VOCABULARY 2

Services

1 Match the verbs (1–6) to the nouns (a–f).

1	decorate	a	a pizza
2	pierce	b	a printed photo
3	frame	c	an air conditioning system
4	deliver	d	your blood pressure
5	install	e	your nose
6	test	f	your house

2 Tick (✓) the most suitable answers. Put a cross (✗) by the answers that are unlikely.

1 alter your …
a skirt ☐ b appearance ☐ c water ☐
2 repair your …
a laptop ☐ b legs ☐ c car ☐
3 dye your …
a computer ☐ b hair ☐ c pizza ☐
4 do your …
a nails ☐ b hair ☐ c neck ☐
5 whiten your …
a ears ☐ b fingers ☐ c teeth ☐

WORDS & BEYOND

3 Match 1–6 to a–f.

1	soy	a	drink
2	minced	b	disease
3	heart	c	sauce
4	blood	d	food
5	junk	e	beef
6	fizzy	f	pressure

4 Choose the correct option to complete the sentences.

1 If you want to lose ***calories*** / ***weight*** , eat bananas – they're 75% water.
2 A banana, like money, doesn't grow on trees you know. It's a type of ***vitamin*** / ***herb*** .
3 You don't have to ***block*** / ***trust*** me on this. You can check the internet – some bananas are red.
4 I have a ***voucher*** / ***petition*** for a 20% discount on a trip to India – the largest producer of bananas in the world.
5 I sold bananas on my Walthamstow street market ***shop*** / ***stall*** for years.
6 Now, here's a nice ***wrap*** / ***grain*** for you: filled with fried banana, onion and spinach!

5 Tick (✓) the kinds of food a vegetarian would eat.

1	beef	☐	6	beans	☐
2	corn	☐	7	chilli peppers	☐
3	mayonnaise	☐	8	minced meat	☐
4	fish	☐	9	soy sauce	☐
5	grains	☐	10	(cooked) dough	☐

Did you know?

Although people say 'banana tree', the banana actually grows on a herbaceous plant. Herbaceous plants aren't woody, whereas trees, of course, are. That's why some people say the banana is a herb. Actually, to be more correct, it's the fruit of a herbaceous plant. You can tell it's a fruit because if you look closely, you'll see it has tiny black seeds.

GRAMMAR 2 *Have/get* something done

Talk about things you pay someone else to do

1 Choose the correct options to complete the grammar table.

Have/get something done
Use: For things you (1) ***pay*** / ***are paid*** or ask someone to do (2) ***with*** / ***for*** you.
Form: *have/get* + thing + past (3) ***participle*** / ***perfect*** *Get* is more (4) ***formal*** / ***informal*** .

2 › Match (1–6) to (a–f) to complete the phrases.

1 have your eyes
2 get your car
3 have your hair
4 get your ears
5 get your clothes
6 have your teeth

a cut
b whitened
c pierced
d tested
e washed
f repaired

3 › Match the sentences to what the person says next.

1 My nails looked awful. ……
2 My computer was so slow. ……
3 The walls were so dirty and I hated the colour. ……
4 I loved the tattoo on my right shoulder. ……
5 I didn't like the look of the spot on my neck. ……
6 All the electric wiring in the house was old and dangerous. ……

a So I got another one done on my left.
b So I got them manicured.
c So I had them painted while I was away on holiday.
d So I got it looked at by the doctor.
e So I got it replaced before I moved in.
f So I got my systems upgraded online.

4 › Rearrange the words to make sentences.

1 having / We're / the / planted / garden / .
……
2 had / our / repaired / computer / We / .
……
3 trained / dog / get / We're / going to / the / .
……
4 kitchen / John and Alice / getting / new / a / fitted / are / .
……
5 Friday / have / I / suit / my / cleaned / every / .
……
6 courier / by / the / parcel / delivered / He / got / .
……

5 ›› Write a second sentence that means the same as the first, using the correct form of *have* or *get*.

1 The plumber came round to fix the toilet for me yesterday.
I had the toilet fixed yesterday.
2 The builder's coming round to knock down my kitchen wall tomorrow.
……
3 The baker's making our special anniversary cake today.
……
4 I asked John to collect the new fridge this Friday.
……
5 The beautician's going to do my nails.
……

6 ››› Complete the interview with the words in brackets. Use the correct form of *have/get*.

Interviewer: (1) *Are you really going to have all your hair cut off* (you / really / have / all your hair / cut off) for charity next week at the PopArts Festival?
Katie: Yes! Last year (2) …… (I / have / my hair / dye) bright pink and I raised £10,000 for UNICEF.
Interviewer: Incredible! Now, speaking of body parts, your teeth look amazing. But … tell the truth: (3) …… (you / ever have / them / whiten)?
Katie: No! (4) …… (I / never have / them / whiten) – honest!
Interviewer: Hmm … OK. What about body art – (5) …… (ever have / a tattoo / do)?
Katie: Not yet, but (6) …… (I / have / one / do) for my birthday this Friday – a butterfly on the back of my neck.
Interviewer: Ah … yes … your birthday. Any nice plans?
Katie: Well, (7) …… (my boyfriend / get / a special ring / make) for me at the moment – a Claddagh ring from where he's from – Galway, in Ireland. And (8) …… (we / have / a big party / organise) by a professional party planner – it should be amazing. (9) …… (we / have / the house / decorate) yesterday and (10) …… (we / have / a huge dinner table / deliver) tomorrow just in time for the special occasion – there'll be over 400 guests.
Interviewer: Wow! Sounds amazing. Am I invited?
Katie: No!

SPEAKING

Ask for advice at the hairdresser's

1 41 **Listen to four conversations. Which hairstyle (A–G) does each person choose?**

Conversation 1 ____ Conversation 3 ____
Conversation 2 ____ Conversation 4 ____

2 41 **Listen again and write the correct customer number next to each question.**

1 Which customer wants a product put in their hair at the end? ____
2 Which customer doesn't want a haircut? ____
3 Which customer doesn't want to change the length much? ____
4 Which customer changes their mind about their haircut? ____

3 Complete the *Phrasebook* with the words in the box.

dried fringe gel good highlights
longer recommend suit top trim

4 a Choose the best option to complete the sentences.

1 Do you think red would ***fit*** / ***suit*** me?
2 I think dark red would look ***smooth*** / ***good*** with your skin colour, yes.
3 ***Would*** / ***Do*** you like some highlights as well?
4 I'm not sure exactly, but I'd like something a lot shorter. What would you ***recommend*** / ***like*** ?
5 I think having the sides and back short would suit you and I could ***smooth*** / ***leave*** it a bit longer on the top.
6 I'd choose ***highlights*** / ***wax*** – it makes it look shinier.
7 How ***much*** / ***short*** would you like me to cut off?
8 I'd ***think*** / ***suggest*** a number two – that leaves you with a quarter of an inch of hair all over.
9 I'd like the fringe shorter and the back and sides ***longer*** / ***trimmed*** too.
10 ***Would*** / ***Could*** you like it blow-dried though?

b 41 **Now listen to the conversations again and check your answers.**

c 42 **Listen and repeat the sentences in Exercise 4a. Pay special attention to stress and intonation.**

5 a Write a conversation between a hairdresser and a customer. Try to use at least six of the phrases from the *Phrasebook* for asking what the customer wants done, and asking for and giving advice.

A: ____
B: ____
A: ____
B: ____
A: ____
B: ____

b Read your conversation out loud, paying special attention to the key phrases. Record yourself if you can.

PHRASEBOOK

The hairdresser:
What sort of haircut would you like?
How much would you like me to cut off?
How would you like your hair cut?
Would you like it (1) blow-____ / smooth/curly?
Would you like anything/gel/wax on it?

The customer:
I'd like a (2) ____ and some (3) ____ .
I'd like the (4) ____ shorter.
I don't want much off the back/sides/ (5) ____ .
Could you put some wax/(6) ____ on it?

Ask for and give advice
Do you think … would (7) ____ me?
What would you suggest/(8) ____ ?
I think … would look (9) ____ .
I'd leave it a bit (10) ____ at the back.

WRITING

Write a report

1 Complete the tips with the words in the box.

REMEMBER HOW TO …

write a report

conclusion headings introduction
opinions subject suggestions top why

- At the (1) ________ , write who the report is to, who it's from and the (2) ________ .
- Use (3) ________ to make the aim of the paragraphs clear.
- Start with a(n) (4) ________ . Say (5) ________ you're writing the report.
- Include (6) ________ : *We agreed*, etc …
- Finish with a(n) (7) ________ . Include (8) ________ with *could*, *should* and with *suggest* + verb + *-ing*.

2 Number the section headings in (logical) order.

1 Conclusion	Paragraph ___
2 Negative aspects	Paragraph ___
3 Subject	Paragraph *1*
4 Positive aspects	Paragraph ___
5 Introduction	Paragraph ___

3 a Match the headings (1–5) from Exercise 2 to sections (a–e) of the report about a local park on the right. (Don't worry about the missing words in the paragraphs yet.)

b Now write the correct paragraph number next to each heading in the report.

4 Complete the report in Exercise 3 with the words in the box.

appreciate benches exercise improvements
picnic provided shade wild

5 Find expressions in the text that do the following things. Write them below.

1 Give a reason for the report (find one):

____

2 Give an opinion (find three or more):

____

____

____

3 Make suggestions (find three or more):

____

____

____

a ________ ________
While we all (1) ________ the park, we believe that some (2) ________ could be made. There aren't enough (3) ________ for people to sit on and dogs are often left to run (4) ________ and could be a danger to members of the public. Also, the lake is full of leaves.

b *Subject* : Our local park *Paragraph 1*

c ________ ________
What we think is that the lake should be cleaned and boats could be (5) ________ so we could go rowing. We also suggest making cycle paths so that young and old people can (6) ________ in a safe environment. Additionally, there should be a rule which says that dogs in the park must be kept under their owners' control at all times.

d ________ ________
We were asked by our teacher to write a report about our local park. We discussed the park in class, and we decided that there are some positive aspects to it, and other things that could be made better.

e ________ ________
Everybody agrees that it's great to have a place that provides (7) ________ in the middle of a hot summer. We feel it's a place where you can meet up with friends and also have a (8) ________ .

WRITING PLAN

6 a You're going to write a report about a public space near you (a museum, square, gallery, sports centre, etc) for your English teacher. First, look at questions 1–5 below. Write them in the best paragraph of your *Writing plan*.

1 What's the subject?
2 What can I say or what opinions do I have about the negative points?
3 What can I say or what opinions do I have about the positive points?
4 What suggestions for improvements can I make?
5 What do I say in the introduction?

WRITING PLAN

Make notes for your report.

Paragraph 1:
Question: *What's the subject?* ☐
Notes: ....
Paragraph 2:
Question: .... ☐
Notes: ....
Paragraph 3:
Question: .... ☐
Notes: ....
Paragraph 4:
Question: .... ☐
Notes: ....
Paragraph 5:
Question: .... ☐
Notes: ....

b Now make notes to answer the questions above.

WRITE AND CHECK

7 Write your report. Then tick (✓) the stages in the *Writing plan*.

Make decisions

1 Complete the tips with the words in the box.

add cons favour information list others trust you

How to make decisions

- Don't worry about what (1) .... think.
- Make a (2) .... of your options, then force yourself to (3) .... one more.
- Find as much (4) .... as you can about your options.
- Consider the pros and (5) .... of your choices.
- Ask for advice from people whose opinions you (6) .... and value.
- Think about what (7) .... really want to do.
- Decide which option has more things in (8) .... of it.

2 a Write one tip from Exercise 1 that would help each person to make their decision in Exercise 2a. Write the number of the tip.

1 I don't know whether to try to look for a job straight after school or go to college. ....
2 I'm not sure about whether it's a good idea to invite my boy/girlfriend to meet my parents. ....
3 I'm not sure what subject to study at university. ....

b Now write what decision you would make in each situation (1–3). Follow the advice of the tip you gave above, and give a reason for each decision.

1 ....
....
2 ....
....
3 ....
....

GET THINKING

1 Complete the paragraph with the correct form of the phrasal verbs in the box.

ask out break up fall out get on go out let down make up put up

I (1) .... her .... in May and we (2) .... a few times. We were (3) .... well together, but then she (4) .... me .... badly on a couple of occasions. We (5) .... and (6) .... because we didn't think the relationship could work anymore. Eventually, though, we (7) .... and I've learned to (8) .... with her annoying habits.

2 Complete the second sentence so that it has a similar meaning to the first. Use the correct form of the verbs in the box.

accuse advise blame forgive offer refuse remind threaten

1 'You stole the money, didn't you, John?'
She *accused* John of stealing the money.
2 'Don't forget to lock the doors, Katie.'
He .... Katie not to forget to lock the doors.
3 'I won't lend you any more money, Paul.'
She .... to lend Paul money ever again.
4 'Kurt, it's all your fault that we missed the show.'
She .... Kurt for making them miss the show.
5 'If I were you, Harry, I'd take the job.'
She .... Harry to take the job.
6 'It doesn't matter, Nancy. We all get angry sometimes.'
He .... Nancy for getting angry with him.
7 'Can I give you a hand with that, Jim?'
She .... to help Jim.
8 'If you do that again, Brian, I'll send you to the headmaster.'
She .... to send Brian to the headmaster.

3 Match 1–8 to a–h to make compound nouns.

1 trouble
2 chewing
3 savings
4 common
5 fizzy
6 volcanic
7 role
8 blood

a eruption
b model
c sense
d pressure
e spot
f gum
g drink
h account

4 Complete the last word of each saying below.

1 as good as g _ _ _
2 as free as a b _ _ _
3 as bright as a b _ _ _ _ _
4 as blind as a b _ _
5 as brave as a l _ _ _
6 as quiet as a m _ _ _ _
7 as fit as a f _ _ _ _ _
8 as old as the h _ _ _ _
9 as light as a f _ _ _ _ _ _

F	N	K	Q	R	D	W	P	M	F
B	E	O	L	G	O	L	D	O	I
H	I	A	T	W	H	B	D	U	D
V	H	R	T	T	I	I	N	S	D
D	Q	B	D	H	U	A	L	E	L
B	A	G	F	V	E	B	Q	L	E
T	O	I	M	X	H	R	D	I	S
H	Y	Z	N	Y	S	D	L	P	F
L	I	O	N	N	I	L	D	E	G

ALL ABOUT ME

1 What makes you feel free?

....

2 What could you do to become fitter?

....

3 What's the bravest thing you've ever done?

....

1 Choose the correct option to complete the sentences.

1 I wish he ***wouldn't*** / ***couldn't*** keep asking stupid questions.
2 If only you ***told*** / ***had told*** me yesterday – I could have left earlier.
3 I wish I ***would*** / ***could*** sing like that.
4 If only she ***doesn't*** / ***didn't*** get so impatient, she would be the perfect boss.
5 I wish you ***would*** / ***have*** let me help you carry that.
6 If only my old German teacher ***had been*** / ***were*** as good as my English one when I was at school.
7 I wish I ***had*** / ***were*** your confidence.
8 If only I ***couldn't have*** / ***didn't have*** to work this coming weekend.
9 I wish I ***were*** / ***had been*** surer of what to do now.
10 If only everybody ***felt*** / ***is feeling*** about us the way our dogs do.

2 Decide which option is the best follow-up sentence for the sentences in Exercise 1.

a I don't know why the sky is blue! 1
b There are so many things I could do instead. ……
c I suppose it takes years of training. ……
d I got really confused with all the verb endings. ……
e But I'm as confused as ever. ……
f I'm going to miss your match. ……
g You always seem in control of things. ……
h But I suppose it's just how she is. ……
i Lifting that table on your own must be hard. ……
j They love us so much. ……

3 Choose the correct option, a, b, c or d, to complete the sentences.

1 I think all children's questions …… be answered.
a should b wouldn't c didn't d have
2 My timetable …… have been rearranged – I thought I had maths now, but maybe it's a mistake.
a was b mustn't c had d could
3 It …… have taken a long time to write your report – it's 10,000 words!
a mustn't b must c had d did
4 A leopard can't change its spots, …… it?
a does b could c can d can't
5 You …… have packed so much just for a weekend trip – you don't need all that stuff.
a should b shouldn't c must d mustn't
6 Perhaps I …… have studied Italian.
a should b can c can't d did
7 I …… have just gone up to a complete stranger and talked to them like you did.
a must b mustn't c shall d couldn't
8 I …… have remembered how important the game was – sorry, I forgot it was the final.
a couldn't b mustn't c should d was
9 On the application form only three choices …… be ticked.
a mustn't b can c mightn't d are
10 Do you think all animals …… be able to live with each other peacefully?
a should b had c couldn't d wouldn't

4 Complete the conversation with modal verbs. One answer is in the negative form.

Leta: Do you think you (1) …… lend me €50 till the end of the week?
Ho: You know, I (2) …… if I (3) ……, but I just (4) …… at the moment. I haven't got that much.
Leta: I (5) …… have been paid, but my boss (6) …… have realised that as I don't have a written contract, he (7) …… do what he likes.
Ho: Look Leta, I (8) …… be able to lend you half of it, and perhaps we can talk to Jill and she could help out too. She's just over there.

UNIT 10 FUTURE VISIONS!

VOCABULARY 1 >>> Talk about visions of the future

1 Match the verbs to the definitions.

1 discover ....
2 launch ....
3 develop ....
4 produce ....
5 create ....
6 design ....

a to send a rocket, vehicle, satellite or other object into the air or into space
b to grow/improve something and help it become more successful/useful
c to make something new or original that did not exist before
d to find out something that you did not know before
e to make or grow something in order to sell it
f to decide what something you want to make will look like and how it will work, and often to make drawings of it

2 Complete the sentences with the correct form of a verb from Exercise 1.

1 Pluto was first .... in February 1930.
2 The spacecraft that took Neil Armstrong into space for his famous moon landing .... on 16 July, 1969.
3 George de Mestral .... Velcro to work in the same way that a type of plant called burdock sticks itself to dog fur.
4 Most scientists today believe that the Big Bang theory explains how the world ....
5 The Spaceship Company is planning to .... several commercial spaceships that will take tourists on trips into space at its factory in Mojave, California.
6 NASA is currently .... a craft it designed to replace the Space Shuttle (which has been making manned trips to space since 1981) at its US test centres.

3 a Complete the questions with the words in the box.

moon planet satellite space telescope universe

1 How many ....s are there in our solar system?
2 When was the first .... launched into space?
3 Who invented the .... over 400 years ago?
4 The Earth has one .... How many does Saturn have?
5 Where does .... start?
6 It is the biggest thing in existence, but how big is the .... ?

b Match the questions in Exercise 3a to the answers.

.... a 1957
.... b 8
.... c 62
.... d It's at least 150 billion light years in diameter.
.... e Outside of Earth's atmosphere.
.... f No-one's certain. It could be Galileo or Lippershey.

4 Complete the text with the words in the box. Use plural forms where necessary.

atmosphere base colony dome galaxy orbit
oxygen spacecraft space station surface

We are gradually getting to know more and more about the (1) .... in which Earth is situated, the Milky Way. Many people have talked about the possibility of forming (2) .... of people on other planets, but the problem is the (3) .... of most planets lacks enough (4) .... for people to be able to breathe. Astronauts have lived in (5) .... that (6) .... the Earth for some time now but another idea is to build a (7) .... on the (8) .... of another planet. This could be used for people as a (9) .... to live in, but the other challenge is building a (10) .... capable of taking people there (not to mention the task of trying to stay alive once it's landed).

Understand links between and within sentences

1 Complete the tips with the words in the box.

REMEMBER HOW TO ...

understand links between and within sentences

as long as	contrasting	results	time	unfortunately

Look for words and phrases that:

- link events in (1) ____________ (*once*, *by the time*).
- add additional or (2) ____________ ideas (*what is more*, *however*).
- show reasons and (3) ____________ (*since*, *consequently*).
- express conditions (*if*, (4) ____________).
- express the writer's attitude (*surprisingly*, (5) ____________ , *curiously*).

2 Match the headings (1–4) to the predictions (A–D) below.

1 MILLIONS OUT OF WORK

2 SPACE TRAVEL BECOMES COMMON

3 PROBLEMS CAUSED BY PREVIOUS GENERATIONS

4 BETTER TRAVEL FOR ALL

THE YEAR IS 2050 ...

A ☐ Despite wars and economic problems, the world has worked as one to make progress on certain key issues, such as global warming. Fortunately, carbon emissions have fallen a lot compared with 1990 levels, mainly because of a global carbon tax and the increased use of solar, wind and wave power. (1) ____ These have been affecting the weather and climate. If humans don't capture some of the carbon and store it underground, the trend might not be reversed.

B ☐ The increasing use of robots and 3-D printing means that many human roles are not needed any longer. Though business systems are now much faster and more efficient, this has resulted in many people being made unemployed. (2) ____

C ☐ Travel is now much cheaper and more energy efficient. More and more people live and work alone. (3) ____ The first major improvement came when computers managed traffic flow. The second was more cars being controlled by machine. Cars can now legally travel at 100mph everywhere and, surprisingly, there are very few accidents.

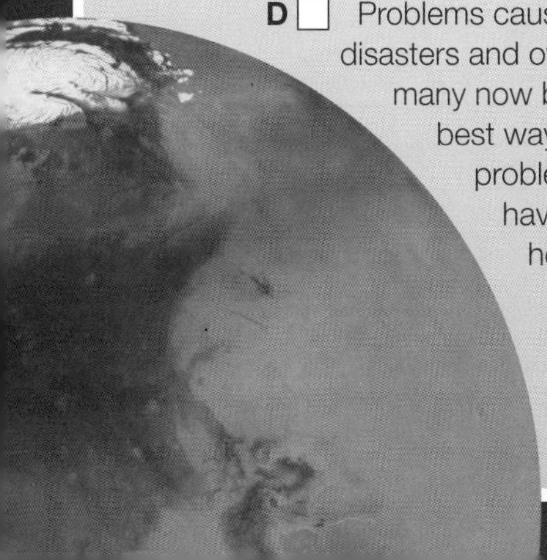

D ☐ Problems caused by environmental disasters and overpopulation mean that many now believe space offers the best way to solve (or escape) our problems. (4) ____ Moon bases have now been established as holiday destinations for the super-rich. And companies are now looking to start mining on the moon and sending solar energy back to Earth.

3 Read the missing sentences below and write the letters (a–d) in the correct place in the text.

a However, carbon emissions from the past are still a problem.
b Furthermore, fewer and fewer people are having families, so most cars are built to carry just one or two people.
c As a result of this, spaceflight has become much cheaper and more common.
d Consequently, crime is also on the rise.

4 Read the text again. Write the linking words from the text in the correct row in the table below.

Time	*first*
Addition	
Contrast	
Reason	
Result	
Condition	

5 Read the text again and think about these questions:

1 Which prediction do you think is most realistic and why?
2 Do you worry about our planet's future? If so, what do you do to try to help?

GO BEYOND

Research other predictions about space and space travel. Think about:

- living on other planets.
- mapping the solar system.
- the limitations of space travel.

GRAMMAR 1 Futures review

Talk about arrangements, schedules, plans and predictions

1 Complete the grammar table with the words and phrases in the box.

be going to   *be likely to*   present continuous
probably/definitely   timetables and schedules   *will be able to*

Futures review	
Use: Different forms express different ways of talking about the future.	
Form	**Use**
(1)	arrangements
present simple	(2) ....
(3)	plans/intentions
will (1)	predictions, often with (4) ....
will (2)	promises/instant decisions
(5)	things that will probably happen
(6)	future ability
Note! You can also use *be going to* for predictions when you can see evidence now, or have reliable information: *Look out! The spacecraft's going to hit the planet!* *A new report says that space is going to be the next big holiday destination.*	

2 Match the sentences to their use in Exercise 1.

1 I will do my homework every evening from now on, teacher. *promise*
2 I'm meeting John at six. ....
3 In the future we'll be able to holiday in outer space. ....
4 I'm going to go on holiday soon. ....
5 English class starts in ten minutes. ....
6 I'll send the email out after the meeting – that's the best option. ....
7 You'll definitely need to pack more things. ....
8 We're likely to learn much more about space in the coming years. ....

3 › Choose the best options to complete the conversation, based on the rules in Exercise 1.

Jo: What (1) ***are you doing*** / ***do you do*** this weekend?
Muge: I have my Italian class on Saturday. It (2) ***'s starting*** / ***starts*** at 9am as usual.
Jo: How about meeting later? (3) ***I'm meeting*** / ***I'm going to meet*** Gemma for coffee at Buck's. We arranged it yesterday – want to come?
Muge: (4) ***I'll try*** / ***I try*** to but I've got lots to do.
Jo: You're always so busy. When (5) ***are you going to be*** / ***are you being*** free?
Muge: (6) ***I'll be able to be*** / ***I'm likely to be*** free in a few weeks. Sorry, it's just really busy at school and work.
Jo: OK, (7) ***I'm texting*** / ***I'll text*** you in a couple of weeks.
Muge: Great. (8) ***I'll definitely be*** / ***I'm going to be*** free then, I promise.

4 › Tick (✓) the sentences that are correct. Correct the mistakes in the incorrect sentences.

1 They'll probably build a new underground train system in this part of the city. ✓
2 I'll definitely to have finished my work by three o'clock. ~~to~~
3 We're be going to leave soon. ______
4 I have to register for all my subjects before the new school year will begins. ______
5 My sister's going to Spain this weekend. ______
6 The train is likely to be arrive soon – it's delayed by about 10 minutes. ______
7 I'll have the steak, please. ______
8 They'll need to work hard if they want to pass this exam. ______

5 a ›› Match the sentences to the responses. Then choose the correct option to complete the responses.

1 The match is nearly over. ___
2 More businesses are spending money on space travel. ___
3 It's too late. ___
4 We are seriously damaging our planet. ___
5 Asteroids keep flying past very close to Earth. ___

a They ***'re going to make* / *making*** it possible for everyone to go.
b We're ***definitely will* / *going to*** need to explore space more to find a new home …
c One ***'s going to hit* / *hits*** us soon.
d England ***are winning* / *are going to win*** the World Cup!
e We ***'re going to* / *'ll be able to*** miss the train …

b ›› Choose the correct option to complete the explanation.

Where the correct answer above is *going to*, this is an example of using *going to* for ***plans and intentions* / *predictions***.

6 ››› Complete each sentence with a future form of the verbs in the box.

create	design	develop	discover	launch	produce

1 I think they ______ definitely ______ the new satellite from the desert – not close to a city like last time.
2 I think we ______ likely ______ many natural resources on the moon in years to come.
3 Several companies ______ spacecraft that will take normal people into space. Some have already started and a few have begun testing their machines.
4 Do you think they ______ things on the moon in the future – you know, have factories there? They can't at the moment.
5 NASA's space shuttles are not in use anymore. They ______ to ______ their new spacecraft to look very different.
6 I've decided I ______ two files – one to write my CV in and the other for my application letter.

7 ››› For sentences 1–6 below, write a second sentence that is similar in meaning to the first one. Use the word in brackets.

1 My sister intends to meet us after the movie. (going)
My sister's going to meet us after the movie.
2 His exam is on the 23rd. (has)
______
3 You can get off the train at Milan. (stops)
______
4 I've booked a holiday – I need a break. (going)
______
5 People will travel to Mars in the future. (able)
______
6 Real Madrid will probably not win the match. (not likely)
______

LISTENING

Understand paraphrase

1 Complete the tips with the words and phrases in the box.

REMEMBER HOW TO …

understand paraphrase

difficult   means   so   who/which/that

Speakers often repeat things in other words to make them clear. Listen for:

- relative clauses ((1) ________).
- sentences starting with *In other words,* (2) ________ , … .
- expressions like *that is, which/that* (3) ________ … .
- repeated words and synonyms (*problematic/*(4) ________).

2 Match the predictions to the photos.

A ☐

B ☐

C ☐

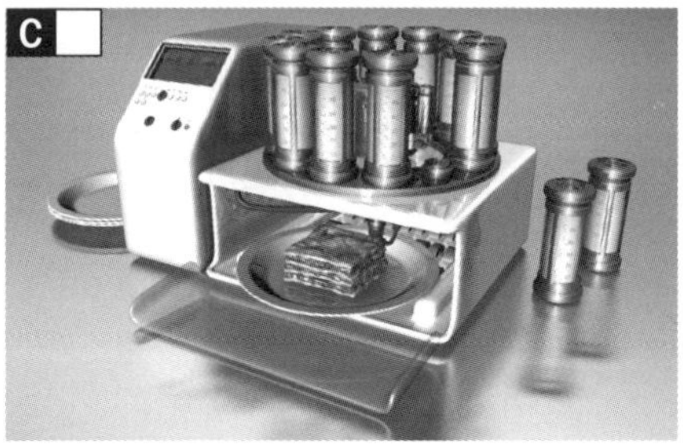

1 People will rely less and less on their cars.
2 We will change the way many of our products are made.
3 People will live in larger towns and cities.

3 ▶43 Listen and number the predictions in the order you hear them.

How we grow things will change. ____
Our energy supply will change. ____
Our jobs will change. ____
Where we live and work will change. ____

4 ▶43 Listen again and match the sentences to the predictions in Exercise 2.

1 We will operate in a smaller area. *1*
2 People won't own cars. ____
3 Energy companies won't be so important. ____
4 More people will work for themselves. ____
5 We will buy food products like milk from our neighbours. ____
6 We will heat our houses from the ground. ____
7 Skyscrapers will become greenhouses. ____
8 A wider variety of products will be sold by small companies. ____

5 ▶44 Complete the sentences with a suitable word. Then listen and check your answers.

1 Vertical farming, ________ is growing products in a skyscraper, will become more common.
2 Self-sufficiency, in other ________ supporting yourself, will become the norm.
3 Entrepreneurs (that ________ , people who start their own businesses) will be more common.
4 More and more people will live in cities. This could be problematic or ________ , but one way cities will cope is by expanding upwards.

VOCABULARY 2

Prefixes of size, quantity and degree

1 Match the prefixes to their meanings.

1 mini ......
2 super ......
3 mega ......
4 over ......
5 under ......
6 ultra ......

a extremely large (in amount or size)
b extremely
c more of something than usual, eg more successful/wealthy/powerful
d too much
e smaller than normal
f not enough

2 Complete the sentences with the words in the box.

bus hero paid sleep star thin

1 Many people think nurses are under.............. and that they should earn more.
2 He was one of the biggest mega..............s in the world.
3 Many super.............. comic-book stories are made into movies.
4 I always over.............. in the mornings and miss my first class.
5 The mini.............. can only carry around 16 people, the driver told me.
6 Do you like my new ultra-.............. laptop?

3 Correct the mistakes in the sentences.

1 Many of China's cities are so big they are called supercities. ....
2 A new thinseries about space exploration is on television for the next two nights. ....
3 Cities have become ultracrowded, with too many people living in them. ....
4 Many people overestimate how much time is needed. They should allow more time. ....
5 We need megacomputers to process all our data. ....
6 Their facilities are supermodern. ....

WORDS & BEYOND

4 Complete the sentences with the words and phrases in the box.

carbon dioxide exploration founder launch pioneer satellite signal vision

1 Mars has too much .... and not enough oxygen for people to survive there.
2 Johannes Kepler, Isaac Newton and Konstantin Tsiolkovsky were among the ....s of space travel as they provided much of the key maths needed.
3 Much modern day communication depends on .... communication.
4 Da Vinci had the .... to imagine many future scientific developments hundreds of years before they happened.
5 Space .... has developed to such an extent that some say we know more about space than we do about our planet's oceans.
6 Blue Origin is an aerospace company started by Amazon.com .... Jeff Bezos.
7 We constantly send a .... into outer space hoping to contact other life forms in our solar system.
8 The .... of the first satellites into space changed much about the modern world.

5 Replace the words in *italics* with the words in the box.

alternatively consists of is profitable progress rate sustain transmit transparent

1 Very little about space exploration *makes money*. ....
2 Some people think we can't *continue to support* mankind on this planet at the current *speed* of consumption. ....
3 Each planet *is made up of* many different substances. ....
4 We can now *send* signals right across the galaxy. ....
5 A lot of people think we need to focus on *being better* in many areas other than space exploration. ....
6 It has been suggested we could mine for resources on asteroids – *or* a different and simpler idea is just to consume* less. ....
7 Some people say that the moon landings were fake and that *clear* wires were used to create the astronauts' unusual movement. ....

Glossary
***consume** = to use something, eg fuel or energy

GRAMMAR 2 Future continuous and future perfect

Say if actions will be in progress or completed in the future

1 Complete the grammar table with the words/endings in the box.

completed *-ing* past participle progress

Future continuous
Use: For actions in (1) .... at a time in the future.
Form: *will* + *be* + verb + (2) ....
Future perfect
Use: For actions (3) .... before a time in the future, often with *by*.
Form: *will* + *have* + (4) ....

2 In each of these situations decide if you would use the future perfect (*FP*) or future continuous (*FC*).

1 An activity you will do while on holiday next week. *FC*
2 The amount of work finished before the end of the month. ......
3 The number of emails sent by a point in time in the future. ......
4 Your activity tomorrow at 10am. ......
5 A prediction for your job/type of work in ten years' time. ......
6 What you think scientists will know about space in five years' time. ......
7 What achievements scientists will make before 2060. ......
8 Whether people will live on Mars in fifty years' time. ......

3 › Choose the correct option to complete the sentences.

1 The world will ***be speaking* / *have spoken*** just 100 languages in 2100.
2 People will ***be learning* / *have learned*** how to control computers within a few years so they won't have to use physical effort very much anymore!
3 Most of the world will ***be living* / *have lived*** in cities by 2040.
4 Computers will ***have replaced* / *be replacing*** people in factories completely before long.
5 People won't ***be using* / *have used*** pens anymore.
6 Sea levels will ***be rising* / *have risen*** by several metres by 2100 according to scientists.
7 Fish levels will soon ***be falling* / *have fallen*** to dangerously low levels, so we won't be able to order cod and chips from the takeaway anymore!
8 People won't ***be using* / *have used*** cars for over a decade in 2100.

4 ››› Complete the conversation below with the future perfect or future continuous form of the verbs in brackets.

Dawn: Hi Karol, it's Dawn here. What (1) .... (will / do) this time next week?
Karol: I don't know, but I know I (2) .... (will not / do) this essay! I (3) .... (will / finish) it by Friday. It's driving me mad. Why do you ask anyway?
Dawn: Well, if you come with me, you (4) .... (will / watch) the match at Wembley Stadium.
Karol: Really? How did you get tickets for that?
Dawn: By the end of this week my dad (5) .... (will / work) for his company for ten years. So they are giving him these tickets!
Karol: Doesn't he want to go?
Dawn: He would but he (6) .... (will / sit) on a beach in Spain. My parents have booked a holiday.
Karol: Excellent! How will we get there and back?
Dawn: I (7) .... (will / stay) with my nan. You can stay as well if you want.
Karol: That would be great. This will be the first time I (8) .... (will / be) to Wembley. I can't wait!

Express hopes, wishes and promises

1 (45) **Listen to four conversations and match them to the hopes, wishes and promises.**

Conversation 1 ......
Conversation 2 ......
Conversation 3 ......
Conversation 4 ......

a to see each other again soon in a big city in the UK
b to say hello to a mutual friend*
c to remember them
d to phone soon

Glossary
***mutual friend** = someone you both know

2 a Complete the *Phrasebook* with the words in the box.

all	do my best	forget	look	pass on	promise	soon	time

b (45) **Listen again and check your answers.**

c (46) **Listen and repeat the phrases, paying attention to intonation.**

PHRASEBOOK

Hopes

We hope you won't (1) .... us.

I hope I'll see you again (2) ....

Wishes

Marta asked us to (3) .... her best wishes.

I wish you (4) .... the best.

Promises

I (5) .... I'll call.

I'll (6) .... to keep Dan out of trouble.

Saying goodbye

Have a great (7) ....

(8) .... after yourself.

3 Look at these conversations. What do you think the speaker might say in each gap?

1 **A:** .... I know you'll love living there.
B: Thanks. I'll try to enjoy myself.
2 **A:** Molly ....
B: How is she?
3 **A:** ....
B: You always say that and never ring.
4 **A:** I hope Mark will be OK.
B: Don't worry – I'll do .... him .... !

4 Look at the situations below. Choose one and write out a short conversation expressing hopes, wishes and promises.

a You won't see your friend for some time. You're talking to them. What do you both say?
b You're worried about your friend John. John's going to live in Spain with Mel. You're talking to Mel. What do you both say?
c You haven't seen someone you care about for a long time but you're talking to a mutual friend. What do you both say?

A: ....
B: ....
A: ....
B: ....
A: ....
B: ....

5 Read your conversation out loud, paying special attention to the key phrases. Record yourself if you can.

WRITING

Present options

1 Complete the tips with the words in the box.

REMEMBER HOW TO ...

present options

alternatively   either   prefer   whatever

- To present options, use:
  ((1) ....) *you could ... or*
  (2) .... *, /Or ... / One/Another option would be (to) ...*
  Would you (3) .... *to / rather go ... or ... ?*
- When options have the same result, use:
  Either way / (4) .... *we do* + the result

2 a Read the text message conversation and number the messages in the correct order.

Chats ONLINE

A ☐
Nothing much. How about going to a gig? Alternatively, we could just go late-night shopping. Either way, I'm happy.

Chats ONLINE

B ☐
Another option would be dinner and then a gig. What do you think?

Chats ONLINE

C ☐
Hi Lucy! What are you up to this weekend?

Chats ONLINE

D ☐
That sounds great. Would you prefer to eat Italian or Chinese?

b Circle the expressions used in the text messages to present options.

3 Complete the sentences with the words and phrases in the box.

alternatively   another option   either   rather   whatever

1 .... we do, I think we should leave early.
2 .... you could come to mine or we could go out.
3 Where would you .... go – Oxford or London?
4 .... , we could just eat in.
5 .... would be to meet near the shops.

4 Use the prompts and the word in bold to make full sentences to present options.

19:30

1 (you / travel / by car or by train) **could**
You could travel either by car or by train.

2 (would / leave earlier) **another**
.... to ....

3 (you / prefer / Mexican or Indian?) **would**
....

4 (we / stay / with my cousin) **way**
....

5 (would / you / stay with me?) **rather**
....

WRITING PLAN

5 Your pen pal's coming to visit you this week. You're going to write him/her an email covering the things below (a–c). Use expressions from the *Remember how to* box to give options. Make notes about these points in point 4 of the *Writing plan*.

a Suggest alternatives for what to eat for lunch the first day.

b Suggest two things you could do this weekend. You don't mind what you do.

c Ask whether the person would prefer to play football or tennis.

WRITING PLAN

Make notes for your email.

Remember:

1 Start your email: *Hi/Dear …* ☐

2 End your email with a closing phrase. Example: *See you soon / Take care* ☐

3 Paragraph 1: Ask about your pen pal / their family. ☐

4 Paragraph 2: Suggest some alternatives for a and b. ☐
Make notes: ....
....
(cover points a, b and c in this paragraph)

5 Paragraph 3: Say something nice about the visit. ☐
Example: *Looking forward to …*

WRITE AND CHECK

6 Write your email. Then tick (✓) 1–5 in the *Writing plan*.

Rate your progress

1 Match the teacher's comments (1–5) to what they want you to do (a–e). Note: if there are words you don't understand, use your dictionary to help you.

1 You have made a number of word formation errors. ____

2 Your paragraphs are not clearly structured and have multiple topics in each. ____

3 You have not used appropriate linking words (*first*, *because*, etc). ____

4 Your essay is too descriptive and lacks evaluation. ____

5 Your register is wrong. ____

a Your writing is too formal or informal for the task.

b You need to have a clear focus and to structure your text well.

c You need to look at prefixes and noun/verb/adjective/adverb choices.

d You need to give your opinion (for example, on the strengths and weaknesses).

e You need to use words to help join your ideas together.

2 a Read about Juan's situation. Decide if the statements below are true (*T*) or false (*F*).

1 Juan doesn't have an action plan. T/F

2 Juan has a way to rate his performance to see if he's improving. T/F

b Are Juan's suggestions realistic? Why?/Why not? Suggest ways to improve them, changing things that you don't think will work. Write your answer in your notebook.

My language level is currently A2 and I need to be B2 by the end of the school year because I want to go on a working holiday to England in the summer (restaurants won't hire me unless I speak good English). That means I've got 20 weeks to improve my level. I'm going to take an evening course and every weekend I'm going to do a practice test for the Cambridge English: First exam. My teacher will mark it for me. At weekends, I'm also going to take an extra exam class. I want to learn 20 new words every day. I'm going to study for five hours every evening and eight hours on Saturdays. I want to be fluent in speaking. I also want to be able to write long complicated essays and to read academic texts.

1 Use the clues to complete the crossword with eight relationship words.

Clues

Across

3 someone you know but not well enough to call a friend
7 someone who comes to visit and stays at your home
8 someone a girl goes on dates to the cinema with

Down

1 someone who lives near you, eg in the same street or in the next house
2 someone you dislike a lot or someone who really doesn't like you
4 someone you go to school with and who has the same teacher as you
5 someone you play a sport with who is on the same side as you
6 someone who is part of your family

2 Number the two sets of sentences in the correct order.

A (Edward's friend) says:

a They went out together for three months. ......
b He felt let down by her lack of commitment. ......
c He broke up with her. ......
d Edward asked Lucinda out. *1*

B (Lucinda's friend) says:

a She put up with his jealousy for a while. ......
b They got on really well for a few months. ......
c But then they fell out with each other because he thought she had another boyfriend. ......
d Then she finished it with him. He took a long time to get over her. ......

3 Complete the sentences with the words in the box.

chemist eyesight florist's hair nails pizza teeth

1 'I'm going to get my .... done in the beauty salon.'
2 'I've bought some flowers from the .... for Mother's Day.'
3 'I got my .... dyed blonde.'
4 'I need to check my .... I can't see that sign.'
5 'Everyone on TV has their .... whitened. Even sixteen-year-old children can look like theirs are yellow by comparison.
6 'I have to stop getting takeaway .... delivered. I want some healthy food!'
7 'Is there a .... near here? I've got a really bad headache.'

ALL ABOUT ME

1 Choose four of the phrasal verbs from Exercise 2 and write sentences about a relationship you have.

....

2 What type of shop would you least like to work in and why?

....

1 Complete the second sentence so that it has a similar meaning to the first.

1 It can take a long time to get over someone when you break up.
If *you break up with someone, it can take a long time to get over them.*

2 I haven't got his number, so I can't call him.
If ____________ .

3 When he goes away on business, I really miss him.
I wouldn't ____________ on business.

4 I hate work – I would stop working if I had more money.
If ____________ rich, ____________ work.

5 I should have started this job sooner to earn more money.
If ____________ .

6 Some things might not be clear, so call me.
If anything ____________ me.

7 I wouldn't like to be famous.
If ____________ it.

2 Rewrite the sentences, correcting the mistakes.

1 If we've some bread, I could make a sandwich.
If we had some bread, I could make a sandwich.

2 He hadn't been angry if you hadn't dropped his phone.

3 If the sea level will rise, there will be floods.

4 I wish someone turns it off.

5 If it'll snow, I'll stay here.

6 If they won't reply today, I'll be angry.

7 If we don't act quickly, it's too late.

8 I wish you listen to me yesterday and took my advice.

3 Rewrite each sentence using a modal passive so that it has the same meaning.

1 They should have banned fizzy drinks years ago.
Fizzy drinks should have been banned years ago.

2 They shouldn't test on animals.

3 They should limit the amount of fat in foods.

4 The people at the party could have eaten less meat.

5 They could have imported less food.

6 They might have travelled less to reduce pollution.

4 Rearrange the words to make sentences and questions.

1 had / have / you / ears / your / pierced / ?

2 hair / cut / have / had / you / your / ?

3 lots / we / to / need / photos / taken / get / of / .

4 the / car / I / have / washed / had / .

5 has / she / the / had / house / cleaned / .

6 taken / pressure / have / had / you / blood / your / ?

EXTRA READING King Arthur

BEFORE YOU READ

1 a Think about when you read *King Arthur* in the Student's Book. How much do you remember? Write the correct name.

Arthur	Kay	Merlin	Sir Ector	the Archbishop

1 .... was a magician.
2 .... and .... organised a contest to see who could pull the sword from the stone.
3 .... was an old, brave and honest knight.
4 .... was eighteen years old and ready to become a knight.
5 .... was taller and stronger than his older brother.
6 .... had forgotten his sword so .... offered to fetch it.

b Match the names to the people in the picture (from left to right). Who's missing?

1 .... 2 .... 3 .... 4 ....

WHILE YOU READ

2 Read the extract from *King Arthur* and check your answers to Exercise 1a. How did the people react when Arthur first showed them the sword? ....

For fifteen summers and winters, there was no king in the south and the people suffered because there was no order in the land. Then, one night, Merlin the Magician came secretly to Winchester. He went to Winchester Cathedral – the great church in the town – and spoke to the Archbishop.

'Tell all the people to come to the Cathedral on Sunday,' he said.

On Sunday, the knights and the people of Winchester came to the cathedral.

They prayed for peace and a good king. And while they were praying, they heard a sound like music outside the cathedral.

The people went outside. In the field by the church, they saw a large stone. The stone was half as big as a man. A bright, metal sword was standing in the stone.

The people could see only the handle of the sword.

The archbishop looked at the stone and the sword. Words were written on the stone in gold letters:

THE MAN WHO PULLS THIS SWORD FROM THE STONE IS THE TRUE KING OF ALL BRITAIN.

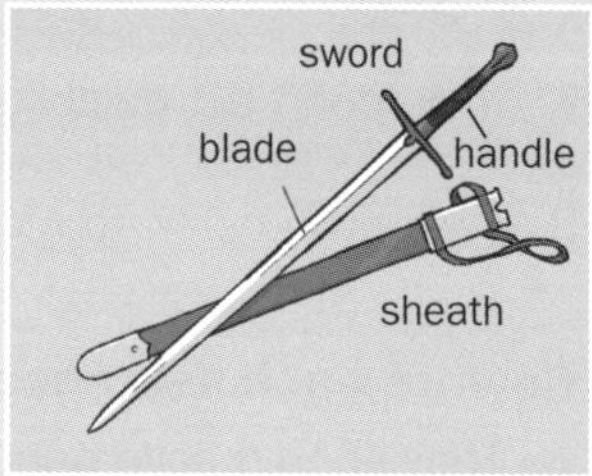

Then one by one, the men tried to pull the sword from the stone. All the knights of Winchester tried, but they all failed. The sword did not move.

'The true king is not here today,' said the archbishop. 'I will send messages through all the lands of Britain. Soon, everyone will know about this sword. Anyone who wants to pull the sword out of the stone must come here at Christmas. On New Year's Day, we will have a contest. We will see who can draw the sword from the stone.'

All the knights of Britain came to gather at Winchester. They put their tents in the fields near the cathedral. It was winter and very cold so the men lit fires to keep warm.

Sir Ector was an old, brave and honest knight. He came to Winchester with his two sons – Kay and Arthur. The three men rode their horses towards the cathedral. It was New Year's Day and they were going to the gathering of the knights.

Kay was eighteen years old and ready to become a knight. But only a king can give a man this title. And there was no king in the land.

Arthur was nearly sixteen years old. He did not look like his brother, Kay. Kay was dark-haired. But Arthur had fair hair, which was almost the colour of gold. Arthur was taller and stronger than his older brother.

Kay stopped his horse. Then he put his hand on his sheath and felt for his sword. But the sheath was empty. 'I have forgotten my sword,' he said to Arthur. 'I helped father to put on his armour but I forgot to put my own sword in my sheath.'

'I will ride back to our tent,' said Arthur. 'The knights are gathering near the cathedral. Go there. I will fetch your sword and bring it to you.'

'Ride quickly,' said Kay.

So Arthur rode his horse back across the field. Then, in the middle of the field, he saw the stone and the sword. The bright sunshine shone on the sword.

'No-one is using this sword,' Arthur thought. 'I will borrow it for my brother Kay.' Then the young man pulled the sword from the stone and took it to his brother.

Arthur did not know why the sword was in the stone. But Kay knew about the sword and the other knights knew too. They all gathered around Kay and Arthur.

'Who gave you this sword?' asked a knight. 'What are you doing with it?'

'Arthur, this sword does not belong to you,' said Sir Ector. 'Put the sword back in the stone. The sword belongs to the true king.'

All the knights watched as Arthur put the sword back into the stone.

'Kay,' said Sir Ector. 'Draw the sword from the stone.'

So Kay put his hand around the handle of the sword and pulled. But the sword did not move. Then all the other knights tried to pull the sword out of the stone, but it did not move.

'Arthur,' said Sir Ector. 'Draw the sword from the stone.'

Arthur put his hand on the sword and drew the sword from the stone easily. Then he raised the sword above his head and the metal flashed brightly in the sunlight. Everyone could see that Arthur held the sword.

Sir Ector got off his horse. He drew his own sword from its sheath and knelt down on the ground. He lowered his head and held the handle of a sword towards Arthur.

'Arthur,' said Ector. 'You are the true king of all the land and I am your servant.'

Arthur was astonished. 'Father, put your sword away,' he said.

'Arthur. You must know the truth,' said Sir Ector. 'I am not your father. Merlin the magician brought you to me more than fifteen summers ago when you were only a few days old. 'Take this child into your home,' Merlin told me. 'The boy's name is Arthur. Take care of him. Arthur and Kay will be brothers.'

When they heard these words, everyone knelt down. Arthur was astonished and could not speak.

Three months passed. At the beginning of spring, Arthur was crowned king in Winchester Cathedral. When the Archbishop put the crown on his head, all the people shouted, 'LONG LIVE THE KING!

3 a Write a simile from the first part of the story (lines 1–35).

....

HOW TO

recognise and understand similes

See Student's Book, page 30.

b Rewrite these sentences to include the similes in the box. Remember to use commas where you need them.

like lightning in the sky	who was as strong as a bear
as fast as the wind	sounding like an embarrassed child

1 So Arthur rode his horse back across the field. ....
2 'I have forgotten my sword,' he said to Arthur. ....
3 So Kay put his hand around the handle of the sword and pulled. ....
4 The metal flashed brightly. ....

AFTER YOU READ

4 a Tick (✓) the things you usually find on the back cover of a book.

a a list of chapters ☐
b quotes from reviews or famous people ☐
c the barcode and price ☐
d the author's biography ☐
e a short description of the first part of the story ☐

b Read about the short description and complete the task.

The short description on the back cover of a book has to give the reader some information about the book and make them want to read it. Short extracts are often taken from the beginning part of the story.
Write a short description for the back cover of *King Arthur* (approximately 60 words). You can use any words from the text.

HOW TO

transfer information to a different text

See Student's Book, page 52.

HOW TO

infer meaning when you listen

See Student's Book, page 42.

5 a ▶47 Listen to Marc and Amy talking about *King Arthur*. Decide if the sentences are correct (C) or incorrect (*I*). Then correct the sentences that are incorrect.

1 Amy thinks the book sounds interesting. ....
2 She doesn't like the cover. ....
3 Marc feels the same as Amy about the cover. ....
4 Amy has seen the film version of the book. ....
5 Amy says she'd prefer to read *Rebecca*. ....
6 Marc and Amy sound like they're good friends. ....

EXTRA READING King Arthur

b Which of these statements do you agree with? Give reasons for your answers.

1 A bad cover can stop me from reading a book.
2 It's good to read the information on the back cover.
3 You don't know if you'll enjoy a book until you start reading it.

6 Complete the *Reading report*. (There is a downloadable copy on the Resource Centre.)

Book title	Genre	Author
Summary (max. 200 words)		
Verdict (What you like and don't like about the extract. Think about the characters and the story.)		
Did you find the extract *easy* (0) or *difficult* (5) to *read*?	0 1 2 3 4 5	
Would you like to read the rest of the book? *yes* (5) *no* (0)	0 1 2 3 4 5	
Would you recommend the book to a friend? *yes* (5) *no* (0)	0 1 2 3 4 5	

EXTEND

7 Do one of the tasks.

Task A
Think of an idea for a new book cover for *King Arthur* that would make everyone want to read it. Make a sketch of your new cover and write notes to explain why you chose it.

Task B
In what ways is the character of King Arthur similar to contemporary action heroes in comics and films? Write a paragraph comparing King Arthur to one or more contemporary characters.

EXTRA READING An Adventure at Brownville

BEFORE YOU READ

1 How much do you remember from the Student's Book? Write one word in each space.

1 Brownville is a small .... in the state of California.
2 In the summer, people often go there to improve their ....
3 The narrator works as a .... and lives in a boarding house.
4 One day as he's walking home through the .... , he hears the voices of a man and a woman.
5 The woman asks if the man is going to murder the woman and her ....
6 The narrator ends up feeling .... of the man. He's dangerous.

WHILE YOU READ

2 Read the extract from *An Adventure at Brownville* and check your answers to Exercise 1. What two unusual things does the narrator discover about the man? ....

There was only one school in Brownville and I was the only teacher. Brownville was a small town and had few young people, but many visitors stayed there in the summer. Brownville has some of the finest views in the state of California. The town lies between hills that are covered in beautiful, colourful trees. In the hills, the air is fresh and clear. Many visitors came to Brownville to improve their health. They walked on the hills and breathed the good, clean air.

I saw many of these visitors because I lived in a boarding house. In summer, the house was full of guests and I talked to most of them. I ate breakfast and supper in the boarding house and spent the rest of the day at the school.

The school was not far away. It was on the other side of a hill. The distance by road was about one and a half miles, but I knew a shorter way. I could walk over the top of the hill in fifteen minutes. There was a path that ran through the forest on the hill.

I came back along this forest path late one evening. It was the last day of term. Tomorrow, the students' vacations would begin. I had stayed late at the school because I had been writing reports.

Suddenly I heard voices. One was a woman's voice, and she sounded angry. The second voice belonged to a man. It was a deep and musical voice — the voice of a singer. I could not see who was speaking, but I could hear the words clearly.

'*Don't* threaten me!' the man said. 'You can do nothing. Don't try to change anything, or you will both suffer.'

'What do you mean?' said the woman's voice angrily. It was a cultivated voice — she spoke clearly and well. 'Do you mean that you'll murder us?'

It was almost dark now, but suddenly I saw the two people among the trees. They were standing on the path. The man was tall and slim. He seemed to be wearing black clothes. But there were too many shadows and I could not see clearly. The woman wore a pale grey dress. They did not see me.

As I watched, the woman knelt on the ground in front of the man. She held her hands together in front of her face. Was she begging for the man's help? Or was she praying that he would not hurt her? I did not like this scene. There was trouble here. I stepped behind a large tree.

When I looked at the path again, the man and woman had disappeared. I walked on until I saw the light of the lamps shining from the windows of the boarding house. The scene of the man and the woman in the forest stayed in my mind. It had made me feel unhappy and uncomfortable.

I saw some new guests at breakfast the next morning. A young woman sat at a table opposite mine, but she was not the woman who I had seen last night.

Then a younger lady entered the dining room. The two young women looked very similar. And they were both extremely pretty.

When the second young lady spoke, I recognised her voice immediately. I had heard it in the forest. The two ladies were sisters. I guessed that they were about 18 and 20 years old.

I finished my coffee and left the dining room quickly.

I did not see the tall, slim man, but I heard him. He was in the garden of the boarding house. As I had guessed, he was a singer. He was practising his singing. He was singing 'La donna é mobile' — a song from Verdi's opera, *Rigoletto*.

The singer had a very good, strong voice. Maybe it was too good. Why was he in a simple boarding house in Brownville and singing in this way? I walked away quickly.

When I returned to the boarding house later, I saw the elder sister. She was standing in the garden with the singer. He was dressed in black clothes. His back was turned towards me, so I could not see his face.

The singer was talking easily to the young woman. I guessed that they knew each other well. When I came into the garden, he stopped talking and turned around. He looked straight at my face.

The man was not young. I guessed that he was about 50 years old. His face was extremely handsome. His hair was thick and black – as black as the clothes that he wore. And the clothes were very fine. They were smart, fashionable and well made. They looked expensive. He could not have bought clothes like these in Brownville. I have seen pictures of opera houses in the fashionable cities of Europe. This man reminded me of the men in those pictures.

The man looked at me as if he knew the thoughts in my head. Did he know what I was *thinking*? The expression on his face was not angry or frightening. But I suddenly felt afraid. Why? I could not explain it. I only knew that I was afraid of this dark and handsome man. He was dangerous. I did not like him.

3 Look at the extract again. Are these statements facts (*F*) or opinions (*O*)?

1 The boarding house was busy in the summer. (lines 12–13) ....
2 The woman on the path was begging for help. (lines 45–47) ....
3 The two women were 18 and 20 years old. (line 64) ....
4 The man was a singer. (lines 27–28 and 69–70) ....
5 The man's clothes were expensive. (lines 88–91) ....
6 The man knew what the narrator was thinking. (lines 95–97) ....

AFTER YOU READ

4 Match the ingredients of a murder mystery (1–8) to the definitions (a–h).

1 setting
2 narrator
3 main characters
4 victim
5 killer
6 witnesses
7 clues
8 suspects

a the people who see the crime
b the most important people in the story
c the people who might have done the crime
d a person who murders someone
e things that help solve a crime
f the person who tells the story
g the place where the story happens
h the person who dies

HOW TO
recognise facts and opinions
See Student's Book, page 84.

5 a 48 Listen to Marc and Amy talking about *An Adventure at Brownville.* Answer the questions.

1 How does Amy describe the setting?
2 Why does Marc think the reader can identify with the narrator?
3 Who thinks the man is the killer – Amy or Marc?
4 Who do they think is another possible suspect?
5 Who do they imagine is a witness?
6 Which page are they both reading in the book?

HOW TO
understand hesitation
See Student's Book, page 86.

b What do you think? Answer the questions.

1 Do you like murder mystery stories? Give reasons for your answer.
2 How do you think *An Adventure at Brownville* will end?

HOW TO
understand the speaker's attitude
See Student's Book, page 98.

6 Complete the *Reading report*. (There is a downloadable copy on the Resource Centre.)

Book title	Genre	Author
Summary (max. 200 words)		
Verdict (What you like and don't like about the extract. Think about the characters and the story.)		
Did you find the extract *easy* (0) or *difficult* (5) to *read*?	0 1 2 3 4 5	
Would you like to read the rest of the book? *yes* (5) *no* (0)	0 1 2 3 4 5	
Would you recommend the book to a friend? *yes* (5) *no* (0)	0 1 2 3 4 5	

EXTEND

7 Look at the picture from another Ambrose Bierce short story called *Beyond the Wall*. Do one of the tasks.

Task A
What do you think *Beyond the Wall* is about? Write the first few lines of your version of the story in the first person. Think about these questions: *Who is the narrator? What's the setting? How does the story start?*

Task B
What do you think is happening in the picture? Write an extract from your version of the story in the third person. Think about these questions: *Who is the narrator? Where is he? Why is he touching the wall?*